Genesis Amidst the Chaos

A One-Year Devotional

Josh Wood

Texas Veritas Press

Contents

How to Use This Book

This devotional was built for one purpose: to get you into the book of Genesis and keep you there for a full year.

Each of the fifty weekly chapters corresponds to one chapter of Genesis, beginning at Genesis 1 and ending at Genesis 50. The introduction and a closing reflection bookend the weekly readings, bringing the total to fifty-two sections — one for each week of the year.

Each chapter follows the same basic rhythm. First, there's the study itself — my personal takeaways from that week's Genesis chapter. I'll warn you up front: I'm not a seminary-trained theologian. I'm a guy from Amarillo, Texas, who loves Genesis, loves Jesus, loves picking things apart, and loves searching for truth — and who spent the better part of a year writing most of these chapters in the margins of a life dominated by caring for a terminally ill teenage son. You'll find real wrestling with God here. You'll find humor here. You'll find tangents. You'll find some science and some history and some pop culture references and at least one passive-aggressive letter from a neighbor. What you won't find is a dry, exhaustive commentary. This isn't that book.

At the end of each chapter, you'll find the AMP section — **AMP Up This Week's Genesis Study** — with three prompts:

Apply — A specific, practical action to take during the week based on what you just read. Not a vague suggestion. Something you can actually do.

Meditate — A question to sit with. These are designed to be honest and occasionally uncomfortable. The goal is reflection, not performance.

Pray — A focused prayer prompt tied directly to the week's theme.

AMP is not a checklist. You don't get a gold star for completing all three. Think of it less as homework and more as an on-ramp — a way to carry what you read out of the pages and into your actual week.

A few suggestions for getting the most out of this book:

Read one chapter per week, not one per day. This is a year-long study, not a sprint. Let each Genesis chapter breathe. Re-read the actual Genesis text alongside each devotional entry — it'll be richer that way.

If you're reading this in a group, the Meditate prompt makes a natural discussion question. The Apply prompt makes a natural accountability check-in the following week.

If you're reading this alone, consider keeping a journal alongside it. The questions in the Meditate section tend to go somewhere interesting if you actually write the answers down rather than just nodding at them.

And if you miss a week — or three — just pick up where you left off. Genesis has been around for a few thousand years. It'll wait for you.

Introduction

Why Genesis?

Years ago when we embarked on our home church journey, I took a deep dive into all things church: church history, denominationalism, traditions, worship styles, structure, theology, etc. Ultimately, I found that many (if not most) American church-goers are quite passionate about a "right" way to do things...which is sort of odd given that almost none of our churches look or feel like the early church in the New Testament. That's probably a whole can o' worms for another day. If you're interested in learning more about our home church journey, search "home church" at joshwoodtx.substack.com. For now, let's talk about preaching.

There are several different theories on preaching. One school of thought is that the preacher should preach through the Bible in a fairly regimented way (verse by verse and chapter by chapter), refusing to deviate from that course for current events or special occasions. Example: if you're a preacher who happens to be preaching through the book of Leviticus and Easter Sunday or some major world event (like war or something) happens to fall on a day when you are supposed to preach Leviticus 13, you stay the course and preach Leviticus 13. You trust that God has the right verse and chapter prepared for whatever may come and whomever may be listening. Of course, one of the downsides to this school of thought is this: you're risking that visitors or congregation members who only come a couple times per year may miss out on the Easter story, Christmas story, or "what Christianity has to say about [insert major world event] and how to deal with it" messages.

Another school of thought is that the preacher should preach to current events and cultural issues each week. Scriptures and passages should be searched out that speak to these things. In other words, preachers should do their best to inject Christ into whatever the prevailing issues of the day are and give biblical guidance for walking through this broken world. The risk with this approach is that it can be easy to avoid difficult passages in the Bible and the difficult questions of the faith. A preacher can preach for 30 years without ever addressing difficult verses, chapters, or even entire books of the Bible.

When we started our home church, I intentionally tried to take on more of a facilitator role than preacher role; but I knew I wanted to move forward with intentionality when walking through the Bible each week. Ultimately, I landed on a more flexible version of the first school of thought. The main plan was to walk through the Bible together — starting in Genesis 1:1. This way, we wouldn't inadvertently avoid the hard stuff and hard questions about our faith. But we'd be flexible enough to allow periodic deviations to address the "big days" of the faith and the historic moments we, as a group, would more than likely live through together.

So, we launched our home church with a plan to start in Genesis 1:1. In addition to a small group of friends who were well-rooted in faith in Jesus, among our first consistent visitors was the atheist son of an atheist scientist. I was immediately tempted to change course...mainly because I didn't want him to feel awkward on day one. Thankfully, I didn't change course and stuck with Genesis. Walking through Genesis 1 (and the rest of the Genesis stories for that matter) with the atheist son of an atheist scientist generated quite the discussion each week. Bottom line: I loved it so much that I decided to walk back through Genesis again — and ultimately turn it into the devotional you're holding now.

As we did in home church years ago, we'll be walking through the book of Genesis chapter by chapter. Call it therapy. Call it accountability. Call it devotional time. In any case, I hope you'll walk with me through Genesis this year. Feel free to challenge the text, ask hard questions, and generally dive in. Perhaps Genesis will bless you as it did me.

One additional note: this devotional has been turned into a chapter-by-chapter podcast and is available wherever you get your podcasts. Links can be found at joshwoodtx.com.

AMP up the Introduction

Apply — Before diving into chapter one next week, take a few minutes to write down two or three questions you already have about Genesis — things that have always confused you, challenged you, or made you curious. Keep that list nearby as the year unfolds. You may be surprised how the text answers its own questions.

Meditate — Consider the two approaches to teaching Scripture described above. Which one have you been most shaped by in your own spiritual formation? What parts of the Bible have you rarely — if ever — seriously engaged with?

Pray — Ask God for an open and honest mind as you begin this year in Genesis. Pray for the courage to sit with hard questions rather than reaching too quickly for easy answers.

Next week: Genesis Chapter 1 — In the Beginning

Chapter One

Week One: The Beginning

Genesis Chapter 1

A few years ago on January 1, I joined many of my fellow Christians in setting one of those "read the Bible in a year" goals. Also like many of my fellow Christians, I failed miserably. But that's not the point. I started out strong in Genesis 1:1. By the end of Genesis chapter 1, I realized that my experience was going to be an entirely different experience than any time I had ever read the book of Genesis in the past. You see, over the past few years leading up to that particular January 1, I had become more and more fascinated with the world of science and physics: quantum physics, the Theory of Relativity, wave-particle duality, the speed of light and other fundamental constants, the origin of the Universe, etc. I've read a number of books on the subject — I'll list a few of them at the end of this chapter. Join me in the nerdery, won't you?

Anyhow, when I read Genesis 1:3 — *"And God said, 'Let there be light.' And there was light."* (NIV) — a couple of things jumped out at me in those eleven words that I hadn't noticed before...things I had taken for granted entirely...specifically, science-y things that seemed to echo the contents of my nerdy books about the theorized origins of the universe.

I should note that scientists who subscribe to the Big Bang Theory (which certainly isn't all of them, but is probably a majority) may disagree on a number of aspects about the Big Bang; but they generally agree on a couple of things: the Big Bang would have been just that — an insanely, ridiculously loud bang coinciding with an insanely, ridiculously bright flash of light. That pretty much jives with Genesis 1:3. I find it pretty cool that the first thing God did in the Bible was speak arguably the most important fundamental constant into existence. But it's the second thing that jumped out at me that continues to fascinate me.

Before I get to that second thing, I need to add a bit of a disclaimer. I've got a couple of business degrees, but I pretty much skipped out on physics in college; and the brain space occupied by any physics I learned in high school was almost immediately replaced by Tupac and Beastie Boys lyrics. Pretty much everything I know about physics today is coming from books I've read over the past few years — more specifically, from the approximately 58% of those books that my feeble mind is actually capable of understanding. As it turns out, there are a very large number of people in this world who are substantially smarter than I am. In addition to that, the Bible doesn't give specifics on any of this stuff, so everything I'm talking about here basically falls into the realm of fun conjecture. Take it all with a grain of salt. That said, let's dive into the second thing that stuck out to me in Genesis 1:3.

For those who know virtually nothing about the Big Bang Theory or any of this physics stuff, let me give you a very brief, non-expertly-worded background. When we're talking about the origins of the Universe or universal laws, Quantum Theory and Einstein's general Theory of Relativity don't really jive. No one is exactly sure why. Many scientists — including Einstein for the latter part of his life — devoted their lives to searching for a so-called Theory of Everything: a theory that would explain and unify the different theories of how the universe works. In their search, they've come up with a veritable cornucopia of different theories. One of these is called String Theory. (You've probably heard of it thanks to the illustrious work of Dr. Sheldon Cooper. Bazinga.)

Here's the basic gist of String Theory: at the smallest fundamental level, all matter is made up of tiny vibrating strings of energy rather than tiny point particles. A long time ago, it was thought that the atom was the smallest fundamental particle — hence the name "atom," from the Greek word *atomos*, meaning indivisible. Then humanity figured out that the atom was made up of even smaller things: protons, neutrons, and electrons. Now we know there are even smaller things than those — like up quarks and down quarks. String Theory surmises that the universe isn't really made up of point particles like these at the smallest level; rather, it's made up of tiny vibrating strings of energy. The vibration of these strings gives rise to the particles that form matter. Different vibrations yield different particles. A bunch of really smart people have done an insane amount of math to establish that this theory has some merit. What's super cool about this to me is that if it turns out to be true, it means the Universe is more like a symphony than a jumble of random atoms. That would mean that, theoretically speaking, the origin of the Universe is as much music and art as it is elements and order.

Back to Genesis 1:3. What if the big ridiculously loud bang in the Big Bang Theory wasn't just the chaotic sound of an explosion of random chance? What if it were far more organized than that? What if it were so organized that it resembled not an explosion of chaotic sound but the boom of something highly intentional? Something like a voice. What if the Big Bang wasn't a big bang at all, but an infinitely loud voice sounding a chorus of perfectly planned vibrations into existence — vibrations that would, from that point on, continue to reverberate and form the symphony of the world and Universe as we know it today?

"And God said, 'Let there be light.' And there was light." (NIV)

After pondering the deeper meaning of life and the creator who shaped the world with a flash of light and a booming voice — with a cadence and a chorus of *"Let there be...Let there be...Let there be..."* light and land and animals and people and joy — and after thinking about the universe as a composed symphony rather than exploded chaos, I had to laugh a little at how relatively simply our brightest minds describe the origins of the Universe. Think about it. After centuries upon centuries of scientific, literary, and verbal advancement, the best description that the brightest minds among us could come up with for the creation of the universe is an almost caveman-esque "Big Bang." How did we get here? Why does the universe exist? *"UUUHHH big bang."* I mean, there's elegance in simplicity and all, but I think Genesis chapter 1 is far more poetic in describing it.

I'm genuinely excited to see what future scientists, physicists, biologists, and theoretical physicists are able to explore and discover. I really hope they keep pressing into the creation story and trying to figure it out, because I think they're just scratching the surface of the complexity of a designer, creator, and composer-God. So if there's a scientist reading these pages — please keep at it. Keep studying. I'm really excited to see what God reveals to you about how this Universe was created.

Further Reading

If the intersection of science and Scripture intrigues you, here are some books worth exploring. A word of honest warning: I neither understand nor agree with everything in them — but I appreciate each author's work and think they're well worth the journey.

- *The Beginning of Infinity* — David Deutsch

- *The Infinity Puzzle* — Frank Close

- *The Language of God* — Francis Collins

- *The Elegant Universe* — Brian Greene

- *The Theory of Everything* — Stephen Hawking

- *A Brief History of Time* — Stephen Hawking *(or try A Briefer History of Time for a more concise version)*

- *Six Easy Pieces* — Richard Feynman

- *The Science of God* — Gerald Schroeder

- *Infinite Powers* — Steven Strogatz

AMP up your study of Genesis 1

Apply — This week, step outside at night and spend a few quiet minutes looking up. Let the scale of what you're seeing sink in. Then re-read Genesis 1:3 and consider: what does it mean that the God who created all of that spoke it into existence with his voice?

Meditate — Genesis 1 describes a God who creates with intention, order, and rhythm — not chaos. Where in your own life do you tend to see chaos where God might be composing something? What would it look like to trust the Composer?

Pray — Pray for the scientists, researchers, and thinkers in your life or in the world who are pressing into the big questions of existence. Ask God to reveal himself to them through their work, and thank him for the complexity and beauty of what he made.

Next week: Genesis Chapter 2 — The Garden

Chapter Two

Week Two: A Suitable Helper

Genesis Chapter 2

Genesis 2 covers a lot of ground, but I want to focus on one verse in particular — verse 18:

"It is not good that the man should be alone. I will make a helper suitable for him." (NIV)

This year I will have been married for 23 years. For me, that makes 23 years of discovering — in a variety of ways — the deep, deep truth of that verse in my own life.

My natural inclination is not adventure. It's safety. It's caution. Had I remained single, I'm confident I would have spent every waking hour holed up in some office, forever working and studying but never serving or living. My people skills would be nonexistent. I'd be an eccentric hoarder of money, information, time, and emotion. Thank God for my wife. When it comes to adventure, she is an icon. She injects excitement into our family. She stretches our comfort zones. She keeps me out of the world of theory and engaged in the much more enjoyable world of trial and failure and success and action. She is my favorite person on this planet. She is my constant motivator.

God knew I needed a helper — and not in the passive, acquiescent, flattering, or subservient sense of the word. No, I needed a helper in the original Hebrew biblical sense of the word. Throughout the Old Testament, the Hebrew word for *helper* (*ezer*) used in Genesis 2:18 refers to God himself as a helper to humanity. Additionally, this word is used in the context of military alliance and reinforcement. So, not only is *ezer* used in the context of God helping humanity, it is also used in a military context. What does this tell me? It tells me that God didn't create Eve because Adam needed a trusty sidekick to help him name the animals or build a tree fort or do his laundry or make him sandwiches. He didn't need a passenger-seat-occupying sidekick for cross-Garden-of-Eden road trips. No, what Adam needed — what humans needed — was a military-grade ally to bring military-grade reinforcement in a divinely inspired way. Because parenting is messy. Because life is messy. It is not good for man to be alone.

There have been seasons in my life when I've foolishly treated my wife as though my life plans mattered more than her life plans. During these seasons, I acted as though she was created to be my helper in a passive, trusty-sidekick kind of way — like a Robin to my Batman. Like a passenger-seat navigator to my driver's-seat trip commander. Twenty-three years of marriage and almost twenty-one years of parenting in the trenches have taught me this: wives were not meant to be resigned to the passenger seats of life. I don't believe that was God's design or the biblical meaning of the word *helper*. I think that's why so much tension is created when husbands assume the role of authoritative delegator — placing themselves in the driver's seat of life as the czar of the family while relegating their wives to the role of the ever-subservient sidekick. Worse, sometimes husbands — myself included — don't allow their wives a seat in the car at all. Instead, we keep secrets. We don't allow them to help. We fight battles alone. That was not God's design either.

It is not good for man to be alone — or to deal with life's challenges, sin, and battles alone. Life is better with military-grade reinforcement, not sidekick subservience. We need someone to help us navigate life. To lovingly confront our messes. To go to battle with us and for us in the literal and figurative trenches. It is not good for man to be alone.

AMP up your study of Genesis 2

Apply — Think about the people in your life who serve as your *ezer* — your military-grade allies. Have you been letting them in, or have you been fighting battles alone? This week, reach out to one of those people and tell them what their presence in your life actually means to you.

Meditate — The same Hebrew word used for Eve as Adam's "helper" is also used throughout the Old Testament to describe God as our helper. What does it say about the nature and dignity of that role? How does understanding *ezer* in its full biblical context change the way you think about partnership — in marriage, in friendship, or in community?

Pray — Pray for your spouse, or if you're single, for the key allies in your life. Ask God to show you where you've been keeping people at arm's length when he designed you to let them in. Pray for the humility to accept help.

Next week: Genesis Chapter 3 — The Fall

Chapter Three

Week Three: The Forbidden Fruit

Genesis Chapter 3

Before we dive into Genesis 3, we should look at the last verse of Genesis 2: *"Adam and his wife were both naked, and they felt no shame."* (Genesis 2:25, NIV)

All was well. Things were good. They were naked and they liked it and life was awesome. And...that lasted one whole verse. Very quickly, Adam and Eve go from naked and unashamed to ashamed and poorly clothed — frantically trying to cover themselves up. The remainder of the Bible from this point on — and post-Bible human existence for that matter — is the story of humanity generally making terrible decisions that lead to a sickening array of devastating consequences.

I do find it a bit ironic how the present time echoes this moment in the garden of Eden. Adam and Eve had this urge to be like God and access all of his knowledge. And they gave into it. They bit the fruit. With one bite, they obtained knowledge of good and evil. And it ruined them. They couldn't control it. It controlled them.

A long, long time in the future, here we are. We're carrying around these devices in our pockets that allow us to obtain, at 5G speeds, the knowledge of good and evil. And they've got these ironic symbols straight out of Genesis 2 on the backs of them — a piece of fruit with a bite out of it. And somehow we think we've evolved enough to control the knowledge now. But the knowledge is still controlling us.

According to a Pew Research Center study, the average social media user between the ages of 18 and 24 spends over three hours per day on social media, while users between the ages of 24 and 65 average around two hours per day.[1] According to another study, the average American phone user spends four hours and thirty-seven minutes per day on his or her phone.[2] As a society, we've invented more means of connecting with people all over the world than ever before in human history. And yet, we feel alone at an epidemic level.[3] By and large, outside of funny cat videos and a few other bright spots, social media isn't making us feel joyful or connected. The social media posts of others are, much like Adam and Eve, making us feel more unclothed and ashamed and disconnected rather than confident and affirmed and connected. Far too often, our own social media posts make us feel the same way when we hit that "post" button just a little too quickly.

I don't know about you, but on more than one occasion I've had a sinking Adam-and-Eve-esque feeling. I post some moderately witty, sure-to-be-hilarious thing on social media, only to very quickly thereafter feel naked and ashamed. One time I spelled the *you are* variant of *you're* as y-o-u-r rather than the correct y-o-u-'-r-e. I've never felt so ashamed. I exaggerate (sort of), but you get the point.

For all its changes, mankind hasn't really changed all that much since the garden. We still get that same sinking feeling that Adam and Eve got — now for over four hours per day. And we still handle guilt the same way they did: blame someone else.

Do you remember Adam's answer when confronted? Adam was like, *um, this woman you gave me made me do it.* Translation: it's her fault — so really, God, if you think about it...it's basically your fault that I ate the forbidden fruit, because you're the one who gave me this woman.

Eve's response was similar: *Um, the serpent tricked me.* Translation: it's not my fault...it's this horrible serpent's fault.

Humanity hasn't changed since then. Don't believe me? Have children. Many kids' first words are "Momma" or "Daddy." But it doesn't take them very long to get to "Not me!" or "He did it!" Of course, we sophisticated adults aren't much better. Who did I immediately blame when I recently broke a rib skiing? Why, I blamed the rock in the middle of the run, of course. Not the 45-year-old trying to be a teenager. Of course not. To paraphrase the great Jeff Foxworthy: you never hear of someone going into counseling and saying, *"You know, my mom was great. My dad was great. My friends were great. I'm just an idiot who makes terrible choices."*

It's just who we are. We're blame-throwers, not blame-owners.

All that said, as I re-read Genesis 3, I find two messages pressing on me personally.

First, I need to spend more time building face-to-face relationships and less time scrolling social media. I need to be mindful that I'm prone to using my phone just like the forbidden fruit logo on the back of it symbolizes — as a gateway to shame, blame, and disconnection from God rather than the opposite.

Second, when I do spend time building face-to-face relationships, I need to stop blaming those people for everything that goes wrong and armchair quarterbacking their lives. And maybe, just maybe, I can start to use technology to help me build relationships rather than letting it isolate me from them.

I'll close with two quotes worth sitting with:

"Everyone is interesting. If you're ever bored in a conversation, the problem is with you, not the other person." — Matt Mullenweg

"It is not the experiences in our lives that change us. It is our response to those experiences. And that should be a very noticeable distinction between the Christian and the non-Christian." — Elisabeth Elliot

[1] *Pew Research Center, "Social Media Use by Age," Statista, 2024.* [2] *"Black Mirror or Black Hole: American Phone Screen Time Statistics," OKW News, 2024.* [3] *Cigna, "Loneliness Epidemic Persists Post-Pandemic," Cigna Newsroom, 2023.*

AMP up your study of Genesis 3

Apply — Track your screen time this week. Most smartphones show this in your settings. Whatever the number is, try replacing thirty minutes of daily scrolling with a face-to-face or voice-to-voice conversation with someone you care about. Also, commit this week to talk to God before you look at your screen each day.

Meditate — Adam blamed Eve. Eve blamed the serpent. Think about a relationship or situation in your life right now where blame is present. Honestly ask yourself: where does your own responsibility begin in that situation? What would it look like to own it?

Pray — Ask God to make you more of a blame-owner than a blame-thrower. Pray for the humility to take responsibility — in your relationships, your failures, and your faith — rather than reaching for the easier exit of pointing fingers.

Next week: Genesis Chapter 4 — Cain and Abel

Chapter Four

Week Four: Cain and Abel

Genesis Chapter 4

Genesis chapter 4 brings us the story of two offerings to God by two brothers. It appears that God liked one of the offerings, but not the other. My translation of the Bible reads like this: And the Lord appreciated Abel and his offering. As for Cain's offering, the Lord was like, "meh."

I have to admit, this is one of those stories I never understood growing up. Both brothers made an offering. It's not like one made an offering and one didn't. Both did. And both were in line with their professions. Why was one better than the other? After reading it again, I think it may have to do with timing. Verse 3 begins with, *"In the course of time Cain brought some of the fruits of the soil as an offering to the Lord."* (Genesis 4:3, ESV) That contrasts with the description of Abel's offering, which is described as firstborn. The picture that is painted is this: Cain, who worked the ground, waited to see how the harvest turned out, used what he needed for himself, and then gave God the leftovers. In contrast, Abel gave the best of the firstborn. He didn't wait to see how his herd would do or wait until the firstborn had kids of its own. He gave first and trusted God for future provision.

Cain's way implies trust in himself. Giving thanks to God is an afterthought.

Abel's way implies trust in God's provision. Giving thanks to God is a first thought.

Immediately after this tale of dueling offerings, we see a timeless picture of human nature. Cain gets jealous and angry. God even tries to calm him down as he wrestles with his emotions. *"...sin is crouching at the door. Its desire is contrary to you, but you must rule over it,"* (Genesis 4:7, ESV) God says. In other words, God says, "I can see what you're wrestling with, Cain. I know you're mad. I know you think revenge will fix it, but that feeling you have—that feeling that revenge will fix everything and make you feel better—it is a lie. It won't fix things. It won't make you feel better. It will destroy you. Fight it. Fight that urge."

Everyone knows what happens next. Rather than contemplating how he could change his own life, he decides it would be better to just destroy another life. Cain gives into the urge. He kills Abel. The pureness of Eden sure did pivot quickly. I've heard it put this way: there were only four people on the planet and the murder rate was 25%.

Yes, it was brutal; but I would argue that things haven't changed all that much in modern times. The acts of righteous people still make us irrationally angry. Wherever there stands someone trying to change the world for good, there always stands someone standing at the ready to crucify her or him. It's a reaction just like Cain's. Our own failures make us mad, and it's much easier to take that out on others than to make a change in ourselves.

On that note, I'll leave you with some advice I heard Dr. Henry Cloud give in a speech once. He is much more eloquent than I; but I'll attempt to summarize his words from memory.

There are three kinds of people in this world. They are classified by how they react to the light of truth. When the light of truth shines upon them, people generally react in three different ways.

The first type of people are wise people. They seek out the light. When the light of truth shines on them, they turn themselves toward the light. They adapt and change themselves and are molded by the truth. Even if the truth is brought to them in a backhanded or poor fashion, they still find ways to apply it to their lives.

The second type of people are foolish people. They see the light of truth and try to turn the light away from them. In other words, they do their best to bend the truth away from them. They make excuses. They blame others. They rationalize. They give every conceivable reason as to why that truth doesn't apply to them. They don't want to change, so they try to change the truth into something that makes them feel good about themselves and their life choices.

The third type of people are like Cain. When the light of truth shines on them, they want to destroy the light. These people can't be trusted. They don't want to hear truth, and anyone who delivers truth to them is going to get attacked. They don't waste time trying to rationalize their choices; they just lash out at anyone speaking truth. They want to destroy truth and all who bring it.

We all know people like all three: wise, truth seekers. Foolish, truth benders. Evil, truth killers.

The point: fight to be a person who bends your life to the truth rather than a person who bends truth to your life. Then, you'll discover one of those great paradoxes of the Bible. Make the truth a slave to you, and everywhere will feel like a prison to you...just as it did to Cain. That was his consequence. But, if you seek to make yourself a slave to the truth as the Bible says, the truth shall set you free.

"So Jesus said to the Jews who had believed him, 'If you abide in my word, you are truly my disciples, and you will know the truth, and the truth will set you free.'" (John 8:31–32, ESV)

AMP up your study of Genesis 4

Apply — Think about how you give. Whether it's time, money, or energy — do you tend to give God (and others) your firstfruits, or your leftovers? This week, identify one area where you can intentionally give first rather than last, and do it.

Meditate — Which of Dr. Henry Cloud's three types of people do you most naturally tend toward — truth-seeker, truth-bender, or truth-killer? Be honest. What situation in your life right now is asking you to bend toward the truth rather than bend the truth toward you?

Pray — Ask God to reveal the areas where jealousy, comparison, or resentment are crouching at your door. Pray for the strength to rule over those impulses before they rule over you.

Next week: Genesis Chapter 5 — The Opening Credits to the Greatest Story Ever Told

Chapter Five

Week Five: The Opening Credits to the Greatest Story Ever Told

Genesis Chapter 5

Genesis 5 brings us the first of many biblical genealogical records.

The Bible is pretty unique in the world of literary works in that it crosses over pretty much every genre imaginable. As we see here, it's a history book and genealogical record. But, at points, it's a book of poetry. At others, a great suspense/thriller novel. At others, a mystery. At others still, a song book. It's a love story. It's a book of the law. It's a how-to guide. It's a prophecy. It's philosophy. It's an epic narrative with heroes and villains and plots and sub-plots and plot twists and cowardice and bravery and sex and horror and greed and indulgence. It's got the worst of humanity and the best of it. It's got wrath and love, injustice and justice, brutality and mercy, judgement and grace, the lowest form of sadness and the highest form of joy. It's rated G in some parts and rated beyond R in others. There's simply no other book like it. It's the greatest story ever told.

That said, when I'm doing my Bible reading and I get to sections of genealogy like this one in Genesis 5, my eyes usually glaze over and my thought shifts to what I'm having for lunch that day or daydreaming about Amarillo's Buc-ee's or thinking about my to-do list for the day.

I like stories. I'm bored by lists of people's names. The more I thought about it though, the more I realized the depth of the significance of these genealogical lists in the Bible. For one, there are about 25 such genealogical lists in the Bible.[1] They tend to mark major moments in Israel's history, and the writers of the Old Testament clearly went to great effort to preserve them for all time. So, God thinks genealogies are significant. Additionally, to this day, there is something inborn in humanity that makes us curious about our bloodline. Don't believe me? Look at humans throughout the generations. We've always cared a great deal about our ancestry and that of others. Falsification of patents of nobility was a rampant problem back in the day. Today, we aren't so formal. We just claim that our second cousin twice removed is related to some celebrity. Also worth noting, some of the greatest sins in human history were committed by people who worshiped a certain heritage...or hated another.

According to Ancestry.com, it has more than 3 million paying subscribers, 15+ million people DNA tested, and 1+ billion searches monthly.[2] To me, that's commercial proof that there is something inborn in us that wants to know where we came from. We want to know our heritage. We want to know our ancestry. Genesis 5 begins to answer that question.

When I read this list of names in Genesis 5, I read it as sort of the opening credits to the greatest story ever told.

When I look through the cast of characters, it's pretty clear that the Bible is guiding me to one of these characters in particular. And it does so using a clever literary technique of an unexpected break in a redundant pattern. Here's the pattern. This guy had some kids. Then, he died. And his son had some kids. Then, he died. And his son had some kids. Then, he died. Then, we get to the 7th name (the Bible has a thing with 7s), and the pattern breaks. Enoch "walked with God; then he was no more, because God took him away." 1 dead. 2 dead. 3 dead. 4 dead. 5 dead. 6 dead. 7 God took him away. It's as if the Bible is saying, "Which of these do you want to be like?" Dead? Dead? Dead? Dead? Dead? Dead? Or, Alive?

Well, I'll take the guy who didn't die. That sounds nice. And the Bible even tells you how to be like that guy. Note what the Bible doesn't say here. It doesn't say: Dead. Dead. Dead. Dead. Dead. Dead. And then Enoch followed all the rules and lived happily ever after. Or, and then Enoch lived a sinless life and God whisked him away. No, in three words the Bible summed up what it takes to avoid dead dead dead dead dead dead. What does it take? It takes actively building a relationship with a God who cares enough about you to enjoy walking with you. Then, take a walk with him. Not a run. Not a jog. Not an email conversation. Not a phone call. Not three prayers a day: morning, noon, and night. No, you walk with God to avoid the dead. It's active. It's personal. It requires a little effort. Then, God will take you away. Alive.

[1] *ESV Global Study Bible, "Facts: 1 Chronicles 6," Crossway, 2012.* [2] *Ancestry .com Newsroom, "Ancestry Surpasses 15 Million Members in its DNA Network," Ancestry.com Holdings LLC.*

AMP up your study of Genesis 5

Apply — Enoch's legacy wasn't his career, his accomplishments, or his net worth. It was three words: *walked with God.* If someone were to sum up your life in three words right now, what would they be? Write them down. Then write down the three words you'd want them to be.

Meditate — The genealogy of Genesis 5 is a long list of lives that ended with "and then he died." Enoch's entry breaks the pattern entirely. What would it look like for your life to be a pattern-breaker in your family, your community, or your generation?

Pray — Ask God to make your relationship with him less like a scheduled obligation and more like a daily walk. Pray for the kind of closeness with God that Enoch had — active, personal, and unhurried.

Next week: Genesis Chapter 6 — Noah's Ark

Chapter Six

Week Six: Noah's Ark

Genesis Chapter 6

Before we get started, I had some fun with AI this week. I asked it to summarize this chapter as a rap song — and I was not disappointed. The rap is available in the podcast version of this devotional at joshwoodtx.com. Enjoy. Anyhow, on to Genesis 6...

We've reached the story of Noah's ark. It's one of the most famous stories in the history of mankind. I grew up in church. We attended religiously — Sunday morning, Sunday night, and Wednesday night. I've heard countless sermons about Noah's ark. Some good. Some terrible. As I re-read the story, here's what I took away this time.

First, Noah didn't have the same luck as ol' Enoch from chapter 5 who walked with God and was taken away. Noah may have even been thinking, "Just take me away!" Instead, he had to build a giant boat and look like a total idiot to all his neighbors every day. I imagine Noah's neighbor, Fred, who lives in the cul-de-sac with him, walks out to grab his morning newspaper. "Whatcha doin' there, Noah?"

"Oh, building a giant boat to save what we can of life on earth when God destroys everything in a massive flood."

Fred: "What? How do you know this is going to happen?"

Noah: "God told me."

Fred: "Sure he did, there buddy."

In a sense, Noah's in the same boat — pardon the pun — that Christians are in today. Because that same neighbor now has Facebook.

Fred: "So, you believe that there was some giant, literal flood that destroyed all mankind?"

Christian: "Yes."

Fred: "Really? How do you know this?"

Christian: "Because it's in the Bible."

Fred: "Ok there, buddy. So, what did all the animals eat while they were stuck on the big boat?"

Christian: "The carcasses of all the dead sinners."

Ok, ok. I totally stole that line from Big Bang Theory. But, you get the point.

For whatever reason, here's what I took away from this reading of Genesis 6: Noah ironically put us in the same position he was in when he built the boat. It's just that I'm not the crazy guy building the boat with no evidence of a storm on the horizon. I'm the crazy guy believing that a boat was built in the first place because the Bible tells me so.

It is worth noting that many if not most cultures have a flood story — *The Epic of Gilgamesh* being perhaps the most notable outside of the Genesis account. To me, the prevalence of flood narratives gives credibility to the event of the flood being an actual historical event. But, I digress.

Here's my takeaway this week: action is important. God told Noah to build a boat. So, he started building a boat. I would argue that modern Christians — myself included — aren't so great at that. Suppose God tells us to do something so outlandish as to build a boat, my first response isn't to grab a hammer. My first response is probably to study weather patterns, research boat-building techniques, form an exploratory committee on boat-building, and see if Tim Keller happened to write a book on the value of building a boat. That's my natural inclination: study, research, plan, prepare. I'm not so much a Ready, Aim, Fire type of person as I am a Ready, Aim, Aim, Aim, Aim, Aim, Aim, Aim, find any excuse in the world not to fire type of person. I don't think I'm alone. I've been a part of a couple churches that are quick to form committees, study groups, etc. but very slow to act. Influx of refugees? Should we drive across town, meet a few people, and share a meal with them? Nah. Let's all do a 12-week Bible study on how to best help refugees. Then, let's form a committee for the service of the refugee community. Then, let's evaluate the committee's ideas. Then, let's pray about it for a couple weeks. Then, let's commission the building of a church in a refugee community. But first, let's put it to a vote of congregation members. Before we know it, we're a year out from an influx of refugees and we have yet to interact with a single one of them in any meaningful way. That ain't the gospel. But, I digress...

Of course, there are a thousand takeaways from the story of the flood; but that's my main one this week. What is one area of your life where God has told you to move and, if you're being honest, you're procrastinating? Is it building a friendship? Repairing a relationship? Engaging those on the outskirts of society? Attending a church? Quitting a bad habit? Is there some area in which you need to stop studying, stop preparing, and just act?

I'll close with this: I read an article recently where Elon Musk decried the "M.B.A.-ization of America." His point was that it can be dangerous for businesses to overvalue those with MBA degrees — who have an intricate theoretical knowledge of business — and undervalue those with real world, trial-and-error experience. It's not that MBA degrees are bad. It's just that A) clean, theoretical knowledge doesn't always jive in the messy real world; and B) MBAs have a tendency to overthink things. Too often, MBAs get stuck in a process of "Ready. Aim. Aim. Study. Aim. Aim. Consult. Aim. Aim." rather than "Ready. Aim. Fire." or even "Fire. Ready. Aim." They spend too much time working on organizational structure and too little time focusing on the product or end user. Sometimes, you have to "move fast and break things" (Mark Zuckerberg) instead of sit at a coffee shop and increase your book knowledge.

Here's my point: just as there is a danger in the over-M.B.A.-ization of America, I think there's a danger in the overthinking, underacting of Christians. Actually, I think there's a danger of the over-seminarian-ization of American church as a whole. But that's another discussion entirely. It's not that seminary degrees are bad. It's not that studying is bad. It's just that seminarians can have a tendency to overthink things — spending too much time working on organizational structure and too little time focusing on the "end user." While I don't have a seminary degree, I do have an MBA. True to stereotype, I'm remarkably good at overthinking, overanalyzing, and generally avoiding action in favor of theoretical contemplation. There's a reason you see the disciples in the Bible learning in an active, "trial-by-fire" type of way. We know by their questions to Jesus that they were nowhere close to mastering theology or debate skills when Jesus sent them out to share the good news town by town. Yet, Jesus didn't tell them to master theology before departing. He said "go." And they went. Just like Noah when he faced a seemingly impossible task, they obeyed. They acted. They built. And God used their obedient action to change the world.

That's my encouragement to you (and me) this week. Get out there and build something. Lean into grace when you fail. Lean into joy when you succeed.

A quote to challenge you this week: *"The early church produced a book of Acts. The modern church produced a book of talks."*

AMP up your study of Genesis 6

Apply — Identify one thing you've been studying, planning, or praying about for a long time — but haven't actually done yet. This week, take one concrete step toward doing it. Just one. Ready. Aim. Fire.

Meditate — Noah looked foolish to his neighbors for years before a single drop of rain fell. Is there something God has put on your heart that you've avoided because of how it might look to the people around you? What would it take to pick up the hammer anyway?

Pray — Ask God to replace your instinct to overthink with a willingness to obey. Pray for the courage to act on what you already know rather than waiting for a certainty that may never come.

Next week: Genesis Chapter 7 — The Flood

Chapter Seven

Week Seven: Being Used by God

Genesis Chapter 7

Here in Genesis 7, Noah enters the ark. Then, the rains came down and the floods came up.

First, some quick thoughts on verse 2. Noah took both clean and unclean animals into the ark. I've heard various discussions about this, so I'm going to address this verse first. Why include the unclean animals on the ark at all...and why have less of them than the clean animals? First of all, clean/unclean does not translate as good/bad. It simply defines which animals are good for human consumption and which are not. Also, it stands to reason that they brought more of the clean animals for A) food and B) sacrifice, as the clean animals are the only ones ok for sacrifice.

Now that those thoughts are out of the way, let's dig into what grabbed my attention in this chapter.

First, Noah got all the way to the end of his life. He'd probably spent a lifetime envisioning how the twilight years of his life were going to play out. Perhaps he'd settle down and retire somewhere near the golf course. Perhaps he'd devote his later years to teaching his craft to his kids and grandkids. What was his craft, you ask? No idea. His entire pre-600-year-old life is lost to history, aside from the noteworthy three words "walked with God" in chapter 6:9 and the fact that he had some kids. There's a lot I can learn from that little fact. No one knows what Noah's occupation was. We don't know what his dreams were, what his aspirations were, or what his career accomplishments were. What do we know about Noah? He did what God asked him to do, diligently; and God used him as a boat-builder and humanity's first sailor.

Here's my takeaway from Genesis 7: there is no time in life that I can get comfortable. God may use me when I'm a kid walking around in the midst of a crowd with a couple fish and loaves of bread. Or, God may ask me to build the Titanic when I'm old and tired and retired. Age is no excuse for saying "no" to God. I realize the following information is secular in nature; but my point is that, if age isn't limiting in the modern economy, it sure isn't limiting in God's economy.

Colonel Sanders started KFC at age 62.[1] Grandma Moses began painting at age 78.[2] Fauja Singh took up running at the age of 89. He is believed to be the oldest man to complete a marathon at age 100.[3] Peter Mark Roget published his *Thesaurus of English Words and Phrases* for the first time in 1852 at age 73 — it would become the most widely used English language thesaurus, with new editions still being published to this day.[4] Mohr Keet began bungee jumping at the age of 88 and became the world's oldest bungee jumper in 2010 at the age of 96.[5] Laura Ingalls Wilder began writing *Little House on the Prairie* at age 65.[6]

My point is this: much like Sarah laughed when God told her she was to have a child at age 100, we too often laugh when God asks big things of us at far younger ages. This year and this time wasn't given to the heroes of old of the Bible. It was given to you. It was given to me. It was given to us. Don't be afraid to allow God to use you to do big things outside of your comfort zone.

I can't help but add another AI rap summary to the podcast version of this chapter. Why? Because this is my therapy session, and these utterly ridiculous raps bring me joy. Find it at joshwoodtx.com.

[1] *KFC UK, "The Colonel's Story," kfc.co.uk.* [2] *National Museum of Women in the Arts, "Grandma Moses," nmwa.org.* [3] *Olympics.com, "Who Is Fauja*

Singh?" olympics.com. [4] *New York Academy of Medicine, "Roget: Beyond the Thesaurus," nyamcenterforhistory.org, March 2015.* [5] *Guinness World Records, "Oldest Bungee Jumper," guinnessworldrecords.com.* [6] *Little House on the Prairie, "History Timeline of Laura Ingalls Wilder," littlehouseontheprairie.com.*

AMP up your study of Genesis 7

Apply — Think about someone in your life who is older and might feel like their best days of usefulness are behind them. Reach out to them this week — a call, a visit, a note — and remind them that God's story for their life isn't finished yet.

Meditate — Noah's pre-ark life is almost entirely unknown to history. His legacy rests entirely on his obedience in one season of life. What does that say about how God measures a meaningful life? How does that challenge or comfort you?

Pray — Ask God to show you what he wants to build through you in this season — regardless of your age, your resources, or how unqualified you feel. Then, ask for the courage of Noah to just start building.

Next week: Genesis Chapter 8 — The Waters Recede

Chapter Eight

Week Eight: Stepping Out of the Ark

Genesis Chapter 8

My family loves to travel. We love road trips. For those of you who don't know me, we have a large family. So, as much as we love road trips, it's always a great feeling to reach our destination. It is not uncommon for our kids to explode out of the confines of the van when we finally park — as if they are experiencing freedom for the first time. Stretching, jumping, sighing with relief. It's a great feeling. I can imagine Noah and his compadres had a similar feeling when the ark door was finally opened after about a year. Freedom.

"Then God said to Noah, 'Come out of the ark, you and your wife and your sons and their wives. Bring out every kind of living creature that is with you — the birds, the animals, and all the creatures that move along the ground — so they can multiply on the earth and be fruitful and increase in number on it.'" (Genesis 8:15–17, NIV)

God basically tells them, "Go. Explode out of the confines of this ark and fill the earth." It's sort of like the first creation when the universe exploded from the word of God. This time, it's a new creation exploding out of an ark. It's like the feeling my family gets when we finally exit the van after a 9-hour drive.

Ok, so that may be over-trivializing it a bit. I mean, the ark full of animals for a year probably smelled about the same as our van after 9 hours, but other than that....sorry, I digress. Back to Noah. He walked out of that ark on an earth that had just been washed from sin. Brutally, but efficiently. And there he walked. Fresh air. Fresh purpose. Fresh mission. Freedom.

The whole thing is quite symbolic. On this earth, we're faced with a choice. Drown in the consequences of our own sin and depravity — or — accept a way out that God has given us. Jesus is the ark. We aren't entering a literal wooden shelter from the storm, but a spiritual shelter of his forgiveness and grace, marked by a wooden cross. And, after we've accepted that salvation from drowning, we are to feel the same sense of freshness and freedom Noah felt walking out of that ark. Every trace of sin, gone. Freedom to walk forward and multiply the gift of God's salvation all over the world.

Here's what I feel like God is trying to tell me: some days, I need to pause and again take that breath of fresh air. I need to stop beating myself up and accept forgiveness and grace. As importantly, what if I worked to live my life in such a way that, when others were around me, they felt that same fresh feeling of freedom? That breath of fresh air. That feeling of yawning, arms stretching, legs stretching, and freedom you feel after stepping out of a car after a long road trip and reaching some beautiful destination. That breath of fresh air and fresh freedom felt after stepping out of that ark after being cooped up for far too long? That fresh freedom and fresh purpose felt after encountering the cross? I want to do a better job of living my life in such a way that those around me feel like that. I don't know about you, but in my life, doing a better job extending that breath of fresh air to others looks a lot like extending more grace and forgiveness.

I'll close with this. I recently read a book by Ryan Hall called *Run the Mile You're In*. In the book, Ryan mentions the importance of celebrating the victories of others. That really hit me, because — confession — I spend far more of my time trying to convince other people to spend their time celebrating my victories rather than looking for and celebrating the victories of others. Perhaps you needed to hear that, too. Be a fresh breath to others in the world. Find someone else's victory to celebrate today.

AMP up your study of Genesis 8

Apply — Ryan Hall's challenge is simple: celebrate someone else's victory this week. Not your own. Find someone in your life who has accomplished something — big or small — and go out of your way to acknowledge it. A text, a call, a handwritten note. Make it about them.

Meditate — Noah walked off that ark into fresh air, fresh purpose, and a fresh start. Is there an area of your life where you've been holding onto guilt or shame that God has already forgiven? What would it feel like to actually walk out of the ark and breathe?

Pray — Ask God to help you be a "breath of fresh air" to the people around you this week. Pray for the grace to extend to others the same freedom and forgiveness that Christ has extended to you.

Next week: Genesis Chapter 9 — Sloppy Naked Drunk

Chapter Nine

Week Nine: Sloppy Naked Drunk

Genesis Chapter 9

The Bible is just weird sometimes. Here you have the ending of one of the most powerful stories ever told — probably one of the most widely-known stories in history. Everyone exits the ark. God gives some instructions and makes a covenant with them. What happens next? How does the Bible follow this epic tale? What does Noah do with his newfound freedom and vision? He plants a vineyard and gets sloppy naked drunk. And, this is the only story of post-flood Noah the Bible leaves us with: a short story about one of his kids seemingly laughing at his drunken nudity — trying to talk his brothers into joining him in the mockery. In case you thought humanity being a trainwreck was sort of a modern thing, the biblical worldview is that we all come from a long line of depravity. Anyhow, stories like this are actually one of the reasons I believe the Bible to be true...because, if you were trying to invent a fable or epic tale, you wouldn't throw weird stories like this into the middle of it. You'd continue the narrative with more great storytelling.

This story does beg the question: how in the world did this story make the cut to be included in the Bible? I mean, I do see the irony in Genesis 3 of Adam eating the forbidden fruit of a tree and realizing he's naked. And then Noah — sort of like a second Adam — drinking the non-forbidden fruit of the vine and not realizing he's naked.

I think there are some moderately disturbing things to ponder there, but here's what stands out to me this week...and I feel it is sort of a cautionary tale for our modern era.

The story gives a pretty good picture of the problem with Canaan throughout history. It's a story of knee-jerk mockery. It's a story of trying to gather the masses to attack, belittle, and demean God's people — both when they make mistakes and when they don't. It's a story of trying to shame people. I think many Christians have felt the shame of Noah. We do something stupid only to have said act of stupidity highlighted by our enemies...or worse, our friends. We're shamed behind our backs. We're shamed on social media. We're shamed in the form of gossipy prayer requests. It's a frustrating place to be: drunk and naked...metaphorically speaking.

Here's the lesson I feel like I needed to learn from this story: it's quite easy for me as a Christian to assume the posture of Ham. To try to use people's bad decisions to heap public disgrace upon them. Social media algorithms even reward that behavior. I think this story serves as a warning for that type of thing though. We're to be people who clothe others with humility, comfort, and grace rather than expose them with mockery and disgrace. If social media is a barometer, I would say that we really aren't all that great at that...especially in the comments section of political posts.

Speaking of trying to be people who clothe ourselves and others in comfort and grace rather than mockery and disgrace...I'll leave you with a few reminders. A few verses where the Bible talks about what we are to be "clothed" in:

"She is clothed with strength and dignity; she can laugh at the days to come." (Proverbs 31:25, NIV)

"...for all of you who were baptized into Christ have clothed yourselves with Christ." (Galatians 3:27, NIV)

"Put on the full armor of God, so that you can take your stand against the devil's schemes." (Ephesians 6:11, NIV)

"Therefore, as God's chosen people, holy and dearly loved, clothe yourselves with compassion, kindness, humility, gentleness and patience." (Colossians 3:12, NIV)

"Meanwhile we groan, longing to be clothed instead with our heavenly dwelling, because when we are clothed, we will not be found naked. For while we are in this tent, we groan and are burdened, because we do not wish to be unclothed but to be clothed instead with our heavenly dwelling, so that what is mortal may be swallowed up by life." (2 Corinthians 5:2–4, NIV)

That's my takeaway from this week: trying to be a person who focuses more on clothing others with grace and dignity and things like gentleness and kindness — rather than mockery and shame.

AMP up your study of Genesis 9

Apply — Think about someone in your life who has recently made a mistake — publicly or privately. Instead of piling on, or staying silent, find one specific way to "clothe" them this week: a word of encouragement, a gesture of grace, or simply refusing to participate in the gossip.

Meditate — Ham's instinct was to mock. His brothers' instinct was to cover. Which instinct do you find yourself reaching for most naturally when someone around you stumbles? What does your social media behavior — especially in comment sections — reveal about which posture you default to?

Pray — Ask God to clothe you with the things listed in Colossians 3:12 this week: compassion, kindness, humility, gentleness, and patience. Pick one of those five and pray specifically for it to show up in a real situation this week.

Next week: Genesis Chapter 10 — Nations Spread

Chapter Ten

Week Ten: Another Genealogy

Genesis Chapter 10

Genesis 10 gives us another one of those lists of names God is so fond of recording. (See my thoughts on the genealogy in chapter 5 if you skipped ahead.) Though it wasn't my main takeaway from Genesis 10, it is worth noting that this chapter is where we see the first mention of Eber, the root of the word *Hebrew*. It means "to cross over" or "to pass through" and is a rather interesting root and word to study throughout the Bible if you're ever interested. It's packed with symbolism.

As for my takeaway from Genesis 10 this week...

We see a whole lot of cursed in the sons of Ham in verses 6–20. In fact, those in his lineage created problems for the descendants of Shem and the nation of Israel throughout history: Egypt. Babel. Canaan. Nineveh. In the midst of this list of names, one sticks out — because he was apparently worthy of expounding upon: Nimrod.

"Cush was the father of Nimrod, who became a mighty warrior on the earth. He was a mighty hunter before the Lord; that is why it is said, 'Like Nimrod, a mighty hunter before the Lord.'" (Genesis 10:8–9, NIV)

Let's step outside of the Bible for a second, because Nimrod is mentioned outside of the Bible as well. Josephus writes about Nimrod and his role in the Tower of Babel. Quoting from *Antiquities of the Jews* by Josephus:

"Now it was Nimrod who excited them to such an affront and contempt of God. He was the grandson of Ham, the son of Noah, a bold man, and of great strength of hand. He persuaded them not to ascribe it to God, as if it was through his means they were happy, but to believe that it was their own courage which procured that happiness. He also gradually changed the government into tyranny, seeing no other way of turning men from the fear of God, but to bring them into a constant dependence on his power."

Josephus paints a picture of post-flood Nimrod glaring at God and almost daring him: *Bring it on. You can't drown us! We're too strong for you.* As you would imagine, this attitude doesn't end well. I'm sure we'll talk more about ol' Nimrod later. Back to my main takeaway this week...

Let's talk about sins that have a ripple effect through the generations of a family. I recently listened to a Matt Chandler sermon where he stated the following: *"You are, for the generation behind you, ground zero. I am earnestly asking God that the stuff that has plagued Chandler men for 200 years goes in the ground with me."*

That statement, for me, was a powerful reminder of the gift Jesus affords us. It's the gift of the death of generational sin through the acceptance of his sacrifice. All that sin bundled up in the guys of Genesis 10 — all that sin that created generational spiritual and physical warfare — it is conquered on a cross. Jesus gives us the gift of redemption and a pivot point for the lineage of the Old Testament bloodlines. If you've read the Old Testament, you'll recall that the book of Kings sounds like a broken record at points:

...and he did evil in the eyes of the Lord as his father had done.

...and he did evil in the eyes of the Lord as his father had done.

...and he did evil in the eyes of the Lord as his father had done.

Perhaps you or someone you know finds yourself scratching a similar broken record.

...and he became addicted to alcohol as his father had done.

...and he treated his wife harshly as his father had done.

...and he scammed people in business as his father had done.

...and he became addicted to money as his father had done.

...and he became addicted to pornography as his father had done.

...and he constantly battled depression as his father had done.

...and he became addicted to fame as his father had done.

I hope you'll find that Jesus is not only a pivot point for generations of Old Testament depravity but also for generations of your own bloodline's sins and shortcomings.

No longer should we add another repeat to our record of the phrase *"and he did evil in the eyes of the Lord as his father had done."*

For us, it can pivot now...and the sins of him and his father were buried in the grave because Jesus said, *"Done."*

Today is a reminder that Jesus came to put an end to familial cycles of poverty, lust, addiction, and so much more. Imagine a world where your ancestors look back at a family lineage of sadness and see you as the turning point for the better. Be the change you want to see in your family...in your kids...in your grandkids.

AMP up your study of Genesis 10

Apply — Identify one pattern from your family's history — a habit, a sin, a wound — that you do not want to pass on to the next generation. Write it down. Then write down one specific, practical thing you can do this week to interrupt that pattern in your own life.

Meditate — Matt Chandler's prayer was that generational sin would go into the ground with him. What would it mean for that to be true of you? What would the generation behind you inherit if the cycle stopped with you?

Pray — Pray specifically for the generation behind you — your children, grandchildren, nieces, nephews, or the young people in your community. Ask God to use you as the turning point. Ask him to bury what needs to be buried and to resurrect something new in your family line.

Next week: Genesis Chapter 11 — The Tower of Babel

Chapter Eleven

Week Eleven: The Tower of Babel

Genesis Chapter 11

First, a little background. We have a brief history of the city of Babel (Babylon) back in Genesis 10. In verse 9, we see that the city was a center of Nimrod's kingdom. Nimrod, a grandson of Ham, fell under the curse of Ham. In other words, not good for Nimrod. Also worth noting: the story of the Tower of Babel is mentioned in at least a few other non-Bible sources — mostly Greek. The narratives differ slightly but share the same theme. According to Josephus, the purpose of the tower was to build something so high that humanity could survive another flood if God sent one. Actually, that seems to be a common theme among the non-biblical narratives.

Back to the Bible. God's call on humanity from Genesis 1:28 was to spread out and multiply. He's pretty clear on this directive.

"God blessed them and said to them, 'Be fruitful and increase in number; fill the earth and subdue it. Rule over the fish in the sea and the birds in the sky and over every living creature that moves on the ground.'" (Genesis 1:28, NIV)

He reiterates it again in Genesis 9:1 — *"Then God blessed Noah and his sons, saying to them, 'Be fruitful and increase in number and fill the earth.'"* (NIV)

— and again in Genesis 9:7: *"As for you, be fruitful and increase in number; multiply on the earth and increase upon it."* (NIV) As fits with the pattern of the Old Testament being physical realities of spiritual truths, we see a similar command in the Great Commission in Matthew 28:19–20, where God wants his message spread out and multiplied. Notably, he does not command them to consolidate and shun the outside world. He commands them to go.

What we see in the Tower of Babel is humanity coalescing to do the exact opposite of God's directive. It's a group of people trying to create one singular location. God wanted the following: spread out, multiply, diversify, go into all the world and spread God's name...spread God's fame. In Genesis 11, humanity instead gave him the opposite.

"Let us make a name for ourselves, lest we be dispersed over the face of the whole earth." (Genesis 11:4, ESV)

Again, God wanted spread out, multiply, diversify, and spread God's name and fame. They gave him instead: consolidate, conform, stagnate, and build a name for humankind. Spread our fame through our centralized power rather than spread God's fame through joyful, faithful dispersion.

Literarily speaking, Pentecost in Acts 2 presents an interesting contrast with Genesis 11. In the Tower of Babel story, God came down and confused the one language of the people in verse 7. Then, they were scattered across the face of the earth in verses 8 and 9. In Acts 2, God came down to unify the people by making all the languages understandable as one. There's more to ponder there; but let's go back to the Great Commission and my takeaway from Genesis 11 this week.

Matthew 28:18–20. Mark 16:15. Luke 24:47. John 20:21. Acts 1:8. The directive is pretty clear. We Christians are supposed to be the messengers of God's blessing to all the world. Alas, we're not always very good at that. Sometimes, we look more like Babel than Apostle. Here's what I mean by that. We sometimes get with our core group of people and build some amazing things. Sometimes it's a business. Sometimes, it's a peaceful retirement. Sometimes, ironically, it's a church. We opt out of diversity across the city/state/nation/world and opt for gathering a bunch of people who look a whole lot like we do to build a giant building that looks like we want it to — it has the kind of music we want, the kind of preaching we want, the color scheme we want, the children's ministry we want, etc.

We Christians (myself certainly included) often buy into an unstated — and sometimes stated — theory: if we build out the right programs, building aesthetics, children's programs, financial structure, and teaching structure, people will funnel into the church. There, they will encounter Jesus. There, lives will be changed. In other words, if we pour our time, talent, and treasure into building an attractive organizational funnel, people will come. If we build it, they will come. I personally have had seasons in my life where I spent the majority of my time and tithe building and serving the funnel rather than directly and relationally serving people.

Don't get me wrong, I think there is a need and place for megachurch-style church programs and ministries. (After a lifetime of "big church" and 5 years of home church, yes, I am *very* aware that many have been burned, scarred, and harmed by megachurches. But, God has changed a lot of lives, fed a lot of hungry people, helped a lot of sick people, cared for a lot of widowed and orphaned people, and saved a lot of lost people who found themselves roaming the halls of megachurches.) Despite all its flaws, the American church model has reached many for Christ and has provided an avenue for authentic relationships for many. So, don't get me wrong, my point here is not that building a big church building is bad. It's just that I think there's a danger and temptation in focusing all of our time and energy on a great construction while ignoring the heart of the Great Commission. Are we focusing on going into all the world; or, are we focusing on funneling all the world into a place or an organization? I could be wrong, but I think Paul would encourage a "reversing of the funnel" in the letter of 1 Amarilloans...and maybe 1 Americans. He might even say something super-eloquent about how a funnel looks a lot like a trumpet when it's reversed.

In a nutshell, that is my personal takeaway from Genesis 11 this week: that I keep a focus on prayerfully, actively, and collectively pouring the love of Christ out on the community more so than trying to build an attractive organization. To put it another way: I hope that, when we Christians part ways after our

Sunday morning gatherings — whether megachurch, small church, or home church — we look and feel more like we're breaking out of a huddle in the midst of a football game and less like we're walking out of box seats of a stadium after the game is over. As much as my Enneagram 3 personality type is tempted to build a lovely, Christianized tower of Babel and spread my own fame, Genesis 11 is a solid reminder for me to make sure I'm not neglecting God's call to go out into all the world and spread his fame.

AMP up your study of Genesis 11

Apply — Think about your current rhythm of church involvement. Are you primarily building the funnel — serving inside the building, the programs, the organization — or are you actively going out? This week, identify one way you can take the love of Christ *outside* the walls of wherever you gather on Sundays.

Meditate — The people of Babel said, *"Let us make a name for ourselves."* In what areas of your life — career, social media, ministry, family — are you tempted to build something for your own fame rather than God's? What would it look like to reverse the funnel?

Pray — Pray the Great Commission over yourself this week. Ask God to give you a specific person, neighborhood, or community that he wants you to go *to* rather than waiting for them to come to you.

Next week: Genesis Chapter 12 — Abram's Call

Chapter Twelve

Week Twelve: Abram Called by God

Genesis Chapter 12

During the days of our home church, we spent quite a bit of time in the book of Genesis. (If you're interested in that story, search "home church" at joshwoodtx.substack.com.) I got so much out of our discussions each week that I frequently find myself reviewing my notes. As I again found myself studying Genesis, I couldn't help but share some thoughts from Genesis 12 — mainly because of the funny story they reminded me of. Without further ado, here we go.

"The Lord had said to Abram, 'Go from your country, your people and your father's household to the land I will show you.'" (Genesis 12:1, NIV)

In a nutshell, this is the call of Abram in Genesis 12: leave everyone you know and everything you are comfortable with. Leave the protection of your father, and go. Go where, you ask? I'll show you later. Do what, you ask? You'll find out later.

So, Abram gathered up all his stuff, and, to his everlasting credit, he went. As he rolled into the land of Canaan, God spoke to him again. God told him that this was it: this was the land that was to be his family's land. Then, Abram continued on his journey. It didn't go well. Seemingly immediately, he encountered a severe famine. I bet he didn't feel blessed. I bet he wondered if he had taken a wrong turn...or heard God wrong...or both.

Personally, I feel like that's how a lot of adventures have gone in my life — especially the things I've been convinced that God has called us to do. Adoption was like that. When I finally mustered up the courage to go where I felt like God called me to go — to take the adoption journey I felt like God called us to take — I felt wonderful as we set out on the journey. I felt that peace you feel when you know that you're doing the right thing. Then, boom. Famine.

We left all of our comfort zones when we entered the world of adoption. We had all the warm fuzzies initially, even as our family went from 2 kids to 6 kids in a matter of 20 months. Life became total chaos. Our house was never clean. Laundry was never done. Dishes everywhere. Shoes everywhere. Milk everywhere. I have tons of stories from those years — many of which I chronicled in my book, *Struggle Bus: The Van. The Myth. The Legend*. Anyhow, here's one fun story that comes to mind.

One day back in 2012, we received a rather passive-aggressive note in our mailbox from someone in the neighborhood. The note's main goal was to condemn the use of our residential home as a commercial daycare. I kept the note. It was a masterpiece of passive-aggressive suburban concern, complete with detailed instructions on proper child supervision, yard safety guidelines, and — my personal favorite — a reminder about commercial daycare regulations. It was signed, memorably, "A Concerned Nabor." Yes. Nabor. Here's the note transcribed from the handwritten cursive (I've kept the spelling and grammatical errors for effect).

This current new clipping from this neighborhood is a shocking reminder how dangerous front yards can be. I shiver every time I see the children in your care playing on your front yard and the babies lying on blankets. And your yard with a circular drive is even more dangerous. Accidents occur frequently:

1. Elderly drivers handicapped with poor eyesight, poor judgement.

2. Divers incapacitated by alcohol and/or drugs.

3. Fools on cell phones taking unimportant messages and texting.

4.   Teenagers racing.

5.   Actual auto accidents where one or both cars careen into the yard from the actual site of impact.

Another danger, these children are on display for any and all child sex abusers that may cruise neighborhoods looking for children to exploit. You are not always in attendance.

Please make a safe and secure area in your backyard for the children to play. Pour a wide concrete walkway to back gate for the kids to use their rolling gear. A swing set, sand box. Secure gates, keep yard clean, and have children "park" their vehicles in an appointed parking area when through with play.

I'm sure that the agency that sets the standards for safe and healthy care of children would not approve of current play area.

Sincerely,

Pucket Area Nabor.

*A newspaper clipping was attached to the letter with the bold headline "**Man dies after car strikes tree**"*

Sorry to disappoint you, neighbor. No daycare here. Just our kids. If we were a commercial daycare, we were the least profitable one in history.

Here's the funniest part. The "babies" our passive-aggressive-note-leaver was referring to weren't human. Our 3, 4, and 5-year-old daughters had set up a bunch of their baby dolls in a school setting in the front yard and had left them there on blankets. Someone saw what they thought were a bunch of living babies sitting in makeshift baby chairs and/or blankets in our front yard for hours on end. Did they come up to our door and talk to us about it? No. Did they call the cops or CPS? No. Did they write a passive-aggressive note to deliver to our mailbox under the cover of night? Yes, yes they did.

Anyhow, the year of adoption was an adorable blur.

It was absolutely the journey God called us to go on, but it sure did feel like a famine immediately after we began. We had no idea what we were doing. We were facing issues we'd never dealt with before. We dealt with humorous challenges like passive-aggressive notes; but, we dealt with real, painful stuff, too. And, God helped us through.

As I re-read Genesis 12, that's what I remember. A journey. A journey where we had no idea where we were going or how to do it; but, we felt as though God told us to go.

I try to remind myself that, just because life feels like a famine immediately after following God's prodding, that isn't necessarily a sign that I've taken a wrong turn. Perhaps you need that reminder today, too. God is there in the famine, and he's there in the feast. We're called to keep moving, either way.

AMP up your study of Genesis 12

Apply — Think about a time when you followed what you believed was God's leading and immediately hit a famine — things got harder, not easier. How did you respond then? If you're in a famine season right now, what would it look like to keep moving anyway rather than assuming you heard God wrong?

Meditate — Abram left without knowing the destination. He just went. What is the thing in your life right now that God keeps nudging you toward but you haven't moved on yet — because you don't have enough information, enough money, or enough certainty? What would it take to just go?

Pray — Ask God to give you the faith of Abram this week — not the faith that guarantees a smooth journey, but the faith that keeps moving through the famine. Pray for someone you know who is in a hard season after doing the right thing, and ask God to encourage them.

Next week: Genesis Chapter 13 — Abram and Lot Separate

Chapter Thirteen

Week Thirteen: Abram and Lot Choose Their Path

Genesis Chapter 13

Genesis 13 is the story of Abram and Lot separating. Abram lets Lot choose which land to take.

"So Abram said to Lot, 'Let's not have any quarreling between you and me, or between your herders and mine, for we are close relatives. Is not the whole land before you? Let's part company. If you go to the left, I'll go to the right; if you go to the right, I'll go to the left.'" (Genesis 13:8–9, NIV)

Of course, one good lesson to take away from this is to try to live your life with a sacrificial humility: to make personal sacrifices to avoid interpersonal arguments. But, here's what resonated with me about this passage:

Sometimes in life, we make it seem as though a decision is absolutely black and white — as if two options lie before us, one of those options will bring with it God's blessing and the other God's curse. We do it with our careers: should I choose this job or that? We do it with big purchase decisions such as homes or cars: should we choose this one or that? We even do it with family planning:

should we have 1 kid or 2? No kids or 9? We agonize over the decisions as though making the wrong one dooms us to a life of misery.

Do you think Abram would've suffered the same fate as Lot had he chosen different land? I don't. I think it was the decisions they made along the journey...specifically whether or not they walked with God or without God on said journey. I think the same can be said for many of our decisions. It isn't so much about whether you choose the more humble-looking house or the more spacious one...or the career with a more lucrative future or the lesser...or the minivan or the SUV. No, it's about inviting God along on the journey and trying your best to remember that it's all God's to begin with. Then, God will bless the journey like he did Abram's.

Ultimately, there are a lot of decisions in my life that I've boiled down to right or wrong, God-blessed or God-cursed.

I remember agonizing over the decision whether or not to move back to Amarillo from College Station, TX. Ol' Lot would've chosen College Station 100/100 times, by the way. My wife and I prayed and prayed over that decision. In hindsight, I'm thrilled with our decision and see many God-given blessings from the move. But, I don't believe that life in College Station would've been doomed to sadness and depravity. No, God could've done amazing, miraculous things there, too.

What's my point? Maybe the story of Genesis 13 is telling me that I was agonizing over some of these decisions for no reason. Maybe there wasn't a right or wrong answer. And, maybe the initial decision was the least important aspect of the whole process. In other words, maybe how you walk the journey is more important than the initial decision-making process. More importantly, if I believe that decisions in my own life can have a lot of gray area in them, maybe I should give a little more grace for the decisions others make about their lives. And maybe, just maybe, when others make decisions I would deem as "wrong," maybe I'm looking at their decision the same way Lot looked at his land — it looks worse to me compared to their other options. But, in the end, God is bigger than my opinion of their decision. So, it's better for me to join people and help them walk with Jesus on their journey than it is for me to gripe about their chosen destination or, worse, to crucify them for it.

AMP up your study of Genesis 13

Apply — Think of someone in your life whose decision you've been quietly (or not so quietly) judging. This week, instead of critiquing their chosen land, find one practical way to walk alongside them on their journey. Bring something to the table — encouragement, a meal, a conversation, a prayer.

Meditate — How many of your major life decisions have you framed as God-blessed vs. God-cursed, right vs. wrong? Looking back, were some of those actually gray-area decisions where the journey mattered more than the destination? What does that tell you about a decision you're facing right now?

Pray — Ask God to help you hold your opinions about others' decisions more loosely. Pray for the grace to invite people into the journey with Jesus rather than gatekeeping the journey based on their choices.

Next week: Genesis Chapter 14 — Abram Rescues Lot

Chapter Fourteen

Week Fourteen: Abram's Choice

Genesis Chapter 14

There's a lot happening here in Genesis 14. On the face of it, it's a story of two men who've had a choice. Abram made a choice in faith. Lot made a choice in logic. Not only did Lot choose the better-looking land, but he didn't do anything with it. He took the easy way out and found a town. At this point, the chapter notes that Lot was "living in the city." So, we know that he has gone from living on the outskirts to living in the city. These choices don't go well for Lot. In fact, he gets caught up in the trouble of the city and carried off in a battle.

Worth noting: the battle was fought amongst tar pits in an area that scholars believe would eventually become the Dead Sea. In other words, the symbolism here is strong. Verse 10 tells us that some fell into the tar pits. So, death is added to these tar pits, which we know were formed from death in the first place...and which would eventually become known simply as the Dead Sea. In other words, it could be said that this was a battle fought in a literal valley of death.

In the story, the godly character charges into the valley of death to fight for Lot, fights for him, and brings him to safety...out of the valley of the shadow of death.

Then, an interesting story plays out. After having survived the valley of death and emerged victorious, Abram finds himself with another choice. This time, the choice isn't which land to take. It's which king's blessing to accept. Two kings. Two options. One a king of righteousness. The other a king of depravity.

Let's first talk about the king of righteousness. Enter Melchizedek. Seemingly out of nowhere, this guy Melchizedek shows up. We can infer quite a bit about him just by his name and title. Melchizedek, King of Salem, Priest of God Most High. That name and title literally means King of Righteousness, King of Peace, Priest of God Most High. Melchizedek offers Abram bread and wine. In return, Abram gives him a tenth of everything.

So, choice one for Abram is to accept the bread and wine along with the accompanying blessing...a blessing that explicitly gives God the credit for victory, not Abram.

Then, we have choice two: the king of Sodom offers Abram everything except the people. *"Give me the persons, but take the goods for yourself."* (Genesis 14:21, ESV) In other words, you can have everything...all the spoils of war...all the accompanying credit and glory.

Abram chooses the bread and the wine and rejects all the worldly spoils of war. Not only that, he is overwhelmed with thankfulness for what the bread and wine represents — so much so that he gives a tenth of everything he has.

This whole story is symbolism that shows up throughout the Bible. Here. In David's Psalms — most notably in Psalm 23 where he walks through the valley of the shadow of death to find a table prepared before him...reminiscent of Melchizedek preparing a table for Abram.

Then, of course, in the New Testament where Jesus becomes the living embodiment of a person who is simultaneously man, simultaneously King of Righteousness, King of Peace, and Priest of God Most High. Jesus, who claims to be the bread of life (John 6:35) and claims that the wine represents his own blood (Matthew 26:28). Accepting his gift is an acceptance of the accompanying blessing that gives God the victory.

Lastly, I think it is worth revisiting Genesis 14:21. *"Give me the persons, but take the goods for yourself."* I think Satan makes a similar offer throughout the

Bible and continues that offer to this day: accept the victory for yourself, the pride for yourself, and all the spoils of war. Just let me have the people. Just like in Luke 4:5–7:

"The devil led him up to a high place and showed him in an instant all the kingdoms of the world. And he said to him, 'I will give you all their authority and splendor; it has been given to me, and I can give it to anyone I want to. If you worship me, it will all be yours.'" (NIV)

All of this can be yours...and you don't even have to go to war for it. Just give me the people. Fortunately, Abram said, "No." Jesus said, "No." And, we need to be reminded to say, "No," too. To our pride. To our wanting to claim "hero" status. To the idea that fame or fortune or success or self-gratification will bring satisfaction and peace in life. They didn't then. They won't now.

AMP up your study of Genesis 14

Apply — Where in your life is the king of Sodom making his offer right now? Where are you tempted to grab the glory, the credit, or the spoils for yourself? This week, practice one deliberate act of giving God the credit — out loud, to someone else — for a win in your life.

Meditate — Abram walked through a valley of death to rescue someone who had made a poor decision. He didn't hold Lot's choices against him. He just went to get him. Is there someone in your life right now who is in a valley — partly because of their own choices — whom God might be calling you to go get?

Pray — Pray over the bread and wine (or grape juice) the next time you take communion. Ask God to make the symbolism of Melchizedek's table — righteousness, peace, and the presence of God Most High — real and personal to you. Thank him that he walked the valley so you don't have to walk it alone.

Next week: Genesis Chapter 15 — A Blood Vow

Chapter Fifteen

Week Fifteen: A Blood Vow

Genesis Chapter 15

Have you ever been far enough away from a city that you can see the night sky in all of its glory? Out where man-made lights don't pollute the power of the light of the stars and planets? There's probably a sermon in there somewhere...like how creation-made lights of stars and planets reach our eyes millions of light years away, but how our man-made lights don't make it outside of our atmosphere. And how light is essentially perpetual in that it doesn't dissipate or "lose steam" in a vacuum but only "goes away" when it is absorbed by the things it hits.

But, I digress. On my first trip to Kenya, we were driven out into the middle of nowhere — an area known as the bush. It was many, many miles from electricity or any source of man-made light. The sky was mind-blowing. You could plainly see the Milky Way galaxy. The constellations stood out as I had never seen them before. I could hardly process how many stars there were...and even the diversity of them all. Different sizes. Different twinkles. Different colors. Different magnitudes of light. That night in Kenya is the mental image I have every time I read in the Bible where God tells someone to look at the stars.

"He took him outside and said, 'Look up at the sky and count the stars — if indeed you can count them.' Then he said to him, 'So shall your offspring be.'" (Genesis 15:5, NIV)

"So shall your offspring be." A diverse multitude of individual lights of various brightness, colors, ages, etc., shining their lights throughout the darkness of both the universe and history...shining their lights throughout the past, present, and future.

I love it when God speaks to humanity like this. When Abram asked for an heir (and a lineage), God could've stuck to words. "Yes, you'll have a son, Abram. And a lot of grandkids. And a whole lot of great-grandkids." But, God didn't say that. Essentially, he said, "Look up. So shall your offspring be." That's powerful. And, the more science has helped us understand about the properties of light and stars, the more powerful the imagery has become.

I can't leave this chapter without talking about verses 8 through 20. Powerful story. Let's unpack what is going on here.

God has just told Abram, "I'm going to give you offspring and a lineage beyond your wildest imagination. And, I'm going to give you abundant land and territory to grow in." In verse 8, we have Abram asking a question...the question all humans ask at some point in their lives: *"Sovereign Lord, how can I know that I will gain possession of it?"* (NIV) In other words, those are great promises, God. But, you seem to have forgotten that I A) have no kids; and, B) am sort of a wandering vagabond with no land. Tell me what I need to do.

God answers somewhat oddly — ok, very oddly — at first glance: *"Bring me a heifer, a goat and a ram, each three years old, along with a dove and a young pigeon."* (Genesis 15:9, NIV)

Humans had this ancient tradition of sorts. It was a way to symbolize a vow between two parties — usually a servant and master or servant and king. They would cut some animals in two halves and lay them out in such a way that there was a pathway of blood between the halves. The servant undertaking a vow would walk the path through the cut-up animals. In essence, the servant who walked the pathway of blood was saying, "If I break this vow, may it be done to me as it was done to the animals I just walked through." In other words, the pathway of slaughtered animals symbolized the seriousness of the vow. You break the vow, you pay with your life.

But, Abram didn't walk through the pieces. God did. In essence, God was saying, "Abram, if you or your lineage don't fulfill this vow, you won't pay with your life. I'll pay with mine."

And, spoiler alert, he did.

AMP up your study of Genesis 15

Apply — Find a clear night this week and go outside to look at the stars — away from city lights if you can manage it. Just sit with Genesis 15:5 and let the imagery do its work. No agenda. No phone. Just you, the sky, and the God who made the promise.

Meditate — God didn't just make Abram a promise — he put himself on the line to keep it. He walked the path of blood so Abram didn't have to. What does it mean to you personally that God keeps his covenant even when we don't? Where in your life do you need to rest in that promise rather than striving to earn it?

Pray — Thank God for being a covenant-keeper. Pray specifically about a promise from Scripture that you are struggling to believe right now. Ask God to make the reality of his commitment to you as vivid as a star-filled sky over the African bush.

Next week: Genesis Chapter 16 — Hagar and Ishmael

Chapter Sixteen

Week Sixteen: Sarai and Hagar

Genesis Chapter 16

This week, we hit the story of Sarai and Hagar. It's that story where Sarai's like, hey honey, how about you sleep with my servant lady? And, Abraham is like, "Well, I can't think of a single reason why that would be a bad idea." So, he does, and gets the girl pregnant, which shockingly makes Sarai jealous. She lashes out at both Abram and Hagar, eventually leading to Hagar fleeing — where she is met by God at a well.

What a weird story. But, there's really quite a lot going on here on a bunch of different levels.

First, I was 40 years old before I caught the parallels between this story and the story of Adam and Eve.

Eve offers Adam the fruit. Take of it and you'll have everything.

Sarai offers Abram the girl. Take her and you'll have all the lineage.

Adam accepts the fruit of the garden. Abram accepts the fruit of the loom. I'm sorry, that was terrible. But, you get the point.

Adam shifts blame to Eve who shifts blame to the serpent.

Sarai shifts blame to Abram who shifts the pawns of guilt off on Hagar.

It's a weirdly similar story. Here's what I took away from it.

It's really tempting to try to help God out in ungodly ways. It's really tempting to try to hit the fast forward button on God's plans for our lives.

For example, the Bible is pretty clear on the concept of keeping the Sabbath holy. Jesus goes as far as to say that the Sabbath was made for man and not man for the Sabbath. What do we do? Honor the Sabbath? Nah, I gotta hustle 7 days per week. Gotta provide for my family.

Proverbs 10:4: *"...the hand of the diligent makes rich."* (ESV) That sounds great, but I'm really looking for the get-rich-quick.

Psalm 46:10: *"Be still, and know that I am God."* (ESV) How about instead I be real busy and act like I'm the God of my own destiny. Like I'm the master of my fate, the captain of my soul.

It's all the same temptation that we laugh at Abram and Adam for.

My point: sometimes, in this American life where we want so badly to hit the fast forward button on our careers, our finances, our ambitions, our dreams, and our relationships, it's really important to remember the false promise of trying to speed up the process by taking matters into our own hands.

Adam and Eve's mistake created an ever-expanding tsunami of brokenness that exploded out of the garden and throughout nature, humanity, and history.

Abram and Sarai's mistake created an ever-expanding tsunami of geopolitical conflict that persists to this day.

Carrying out God's plans in ways contrary to his instruction has consequences. Of course, there are a thousand ways this can play out. I'm just picking on the Sabbath because, well, the American Dream sometimes tries to kill it; and it is something I personally struggle with. I'll leave you with these three quotes to ponder this week:

"Most of the things we need to be most fully alive never come in busyness. They grow in rest." — Mark Buchanan

"Our patterns of work and rest reveal what we believe to be true about God and ourselves. God alone requires no limits on his activity. To rest is to acknowledge that we humans are limited by design. We are created for rest just as surely as we are created for labor. An inability or unwillingness to cease from our labors is a

confession of unbelief, an admission that we view ourselves as creator and sustainer of our own universes." — Jen Wilkin

"Sabbath is that uncluttered time and space in which we can distance ourselves from our own activities enough to see what God is doing." — Eugene Peterson

AMP up your study of Genesis 16

Apply — Pick one day this week — or even half a day — and practice an intentional Sabbath. No work. No hustle. No scrolling. Just rest, worship, and presence. Notice what comes up when you stop trying to be the master of your own fate for a few hours.

Meditate — Where in your life are you currently trying to "help God out" by taking matters into your own hands? Is there a situation where you're hitting the fast forward button on something God may be asking you to wait on? What would it look like to put the remote down?

Pray — Pray specifically about rest this week. Ask God to reveal where busyness has become a substitute for trust. Pray for the courage to be still and know that he is God and you are not.

Next week: Genesis Chapter 17 — Silence and Circumcision

Chapter Seventeen

Week Seventeen: Silence and Circumcision

Genesis Chapter 17

Today, we're going to talk a little about the silence of God and circumcision. Sounds like a great combination, right?

Chapter 17 picks up 13 years after chapter 16. Thirteen years after the birth of Ishmael. For all we know, God was silent during this time. Of course, we don't know this for sure...which means that what I'm about to say is conjecture, not scripture. So, take this with a grain of salt. Let's suppose that Abram spent 13 years at the tail end of his life hoping, wondering, and waiting in the silence of God...wondering about a promise that was originally made to him around 30 years prior. That's a long time. Personally, I would've found a way to rationalize that God had changed his mind over 13 years of silence, especially after the whole sleeping-with-the-maidservant debacle. I probably would've been resigned to the idea that I could die any day without seeing God's promise fulfilled.

Here's a great thing about Christianity and the Bible as a whole: God does not remain silent. As I type this, we continue our 24/7 fight for the life of our wonderful son. Our battle began 05/04/2019. It has grown more challenging every year. There have been many times where I didn't believe I could wait another second on God to show up. I've yelled out, "Where are you in this mess, God?!" and some version of, "How long, Oh Lord? How long?" Plenty of times, my cries have been answered with silence in the form of continued torture. Another seizure begins. The oxygen alarm blares. Isaiah's trach becomes clogged. Sleep evades us. Thankfully, those moments are not the prevailing theme of our post-2019 life. In the midst of the pain, we often feel the calm, peace, and joy of the presence of God — sort of how I imagine Daniel must have felt in the lion's den...or how Shadrach, Meshach, and Abednego must have felt amongst the flames. But, if I'm honest, I haven't had the booming voice of God talk to me and reiterate his promises in a Genesis 17-type way. So, why believe in a God who allows such pain?

For starters, Christ didn't promise me the total healing of my son. (Actually, he warned all of his followers, *"In this world you will have trouble."*) My hope isn't in my perfect vision for my perfect life. My hope is as follows...and I would extend this hope to all of us who've experienced a "9" or a "10" on the 1-10 pain scale of life. Pain, suffering, and darkness — they all have an expiration date. The second verse of the Bible, Genesis 1:2, paints a picture of a dark, empty void (which is sort of how life feels at times); but it also builds hope and anticipation...the hope of a hovering Spirit.

"Now the earth was formless and empty, darkness was over the surface of the deep, and the Spirit of God was hovering over the waters." (Genesis 1:2, NIV)

It's as if the Spirit of God is hovering in a holding pattern there over the darkness, void, emptiness, inky blackness...whatever you choose to call it. Then, God speaks. Out of the empty and eerie quiet, sound bursts forth. God's voice booms. "Let there be light." In an instant, the Spirit moves — like a strike of lightning or rush of a flame into the void. The wait is over. God's plan explodes into motion. Love strikes the emptiness. Light. Creation. Life. Order. Goodness. Joy. A chorus follows for the rest of chapter 1. *"And God saw that it was good."* ... *"And God saw that it was good."* ... *"And God saw that it was good."* ... *"It was very good."*

A rush of order, meaning, and love was injected into chaos and emptiness.

The New Testament tells a similar creation story. Actually, the New Testament contains many similar stories...where, in an instant, love strikes emptiness.

I bet Abraham felt a bit of Genesis 1 joy when God broke the silence in Genesis 17.

When the hovering ends...when joy comes, I think those of us who've experienced a "9" or a "10" on the 1-10 pain scale of life will have a deeper appreciation for the "10" on the joy scale of life. Actually, I think that those of us who have experienced the deepest pains of this life are in for unimaginable joy when the time for hovering is over. 10 out of 10. Perhaps you can't even comprehend a "10" of joy if you haven't experienced a "10" of pain. I don't know.

At some point, the time for the Spirit hovering over the chaos and emptiness of life on this earth will be over. The silence of God — real or perceived — will end. That moment will come. The Spirit, in God's perfect timing, will strike the void. The power of redemption, order, love, meaning, and all the Galatians 5:22 things will strike the emptiness of your life and mine. This weird gap we all live in — the gap between the fall of man and the redemption of all things — will end one day. "The hovering" will be over. Pure joy will come. I pray for that moment every day. Hopefully, it will come sooner than 13 years. Hopefully, during this life. Certainly, it will come during the next. It may come through miraculous healing. It may come through a long road to recovery. It may be delivered through death. We aren't promised a specific time; but we are promised that love will strike the emptiness and chaos in our life. Until then, we pray and wait.

"Everything sad is going to come untrue and it will somehow be greater for having been broken and lost." — Tim Keller

I've decided that the English language does not contain adequate words to create a graceful transition from all that to the topic of circumcision. Also, I'm too lazy to figure it out. Sorry. But, I can't help but at least mention the topic here. Again, sorry.

"This is my covenant, which you shall keep, between me and you and your offspring after you: Every male among you shall be circumcised." (Genesis 17:10, NIV)

Circumcision is mentioned throughout the Old and New Testament. If you're thinking to yourself, "You know, I think I'd love to do a deep dive on circumcision today," here are a few passages worth exploring: Galatians 5:19–21, Ephesians 2:3, Romans 2:28–29, Colossians 2:9–12, and Galatians 6:12–15.

Anyhow, what a weird command, right? Why such an emphasis on this? Why this at all? Why not something more normal...like "all followers of God shall henceforth wear yellow hats, so everyone will recognize you're my people. Thus sayeth the Lord."? Or Christian fish tattoos? Or maybe buddy bands or something? Well, I have some ideas. For starters, it's the cutting off of the flesh — symbolic of the hidden, intimate, sinful nature. It's the cutting off of those deep-down sinful things that the Bible often refers to as "the flesh" — things that don't really stand between you and others but do stand between you and God. It's those things that others don't know and may never know about you. It's those things that are the most difficult to release to God.

Have you ever sat in a Sunday school class where all the prayer requests are consistently non-personal? "Please pray for my grandma's ailment." "Pray for my neighbor's dog." "Pray for my cousin's soul." "Pray for something I can't share but God knows." Week after week of surface-level requests?

Have you ever sat there and thought, "Ok, we'll pray for your 93-year-old grandma's arthritis again, John; but maybe we should also pray for your alcoholic, adultering soul that no one ever seems to confront you about."? Circumcision, I think, is symbolic of things sort of like that...those things we hold onto in secret...those things that some people may know but most don't...those things for which we say, "I'll submit everything in my life to you, God...except this one thing. I'm not giving you this one thing, God. It's too personal. It's too painful. I'll just deal with it myself."

That's what I leave you with today: God wants a relationship with you where you take drastic action to remove the sin in your life that no one else but you knows about. Find a support group. Call a hotline. Reach out to a friend. Call a mentor. Then, march forward with the God who loves you and heals.

AMP up your study of Genesis 17

Apply — If you're in a season of silence — waiting on God, wondering if he's still there — write down the last time you clearly felt his presence or saw his hand at work. Keep that record close this week. The hovering always ends.

Meditate — What is your "except this one thing"? What's the hidden thing you've been unwilling to release to God — the thing that stands between you and him that no one in your Sunday school class or group of friends knows about? You don't have to tell anyone else. But be honest with yourself and with God about it.

Pray — If you are carrying a weight of pain right now, pray the words of Psalm 13:1 — *"How long, Lord? Will you forget me forever?"* — and keep reading through to verse 6. Let the Psalms teach you how to pray honestly in the silence. Then, pray for someone else you know who is struggling in their own darkness right now.

Next week: Genesis Chapter 18 — God and Man Discuss Theology

Chapter Eighteen

Week Eighteen: God and Man Discuss Theology

Genesis Chapter 18

Genesis 18 contains one of the first theological discussions between God and man. Abraham starts out with a feeling of injustice...which is interesting in and of itself. I mean, theologically speaking, the Bible has thus far established that there is one eternal, all-powerful God, creator of the universe and everything in it. Ergo, God makes the rules. If he'd decided that people with brown eyes had to be the servants of people with blue eyes or be smote from the earth altogether, I mean that would really stink, but you can't argue with an eternal God. I mean, you could, but what would be the point?

In the words of Vernon McGee: *"This is God's universe, and God does things his way. You may have a better way, but you don't have a universe."*

Let's jump to God and Abraham's conversation. I'll pick it up in verse 20:

"Then the Lord said, 'The outcry against Sodom and Gomorrah is so great and their sin so grievous that I will go down and see if what they have done is as bad as the outcry that has reached me. If not, I will know.' The men turned away

and went toward Sodom, but Abraham remained standing before the Lord. Then Abraham approached him and said: 'Will you sweep away the righteous with the wicked? What if there are fifty righteous people in the city? Will you really sweep it away and not spare the place for the sake of the fifty righteous people in it? Far be it from you to do such a thing — to kill the righteous with the wicked, treating the righteous and the wicked alike. Far be it from you! Will not the Judge of all the earth do right?'" (Genesis 18:20–25, NIV)

Abraham's sort of saying, "Hey God, I know you're God, but something just isn't sitting right with me. I don't get it. It doesn't really feel right that you would kill innocent people because of the badness of other people. Would you really do that?" You can sense the wheels turning in Abraham's head. "How does all this work, theologically speaking? Does God punish people for the sins of others...and does God save people due to the righteousness of others? For the sake of my family, I've got to know."

Let's take a quick sidebar on verses 23 and 24. Here, Abraham asks God, *"Will you sweep away the righteous with the wicked? What if there are fifty righteous people in the city? Will you really sweep it away and not spare the place for the sake of the fifty righteous people in it?"* (Genesis 18:23–24, NIV)

Suppose God had answered Abraham as follows: "Yep. I'm angry. There may be some good people there, but their entire society is all kinds of messed up. Actually, Abraham, you go kill them all. I'm busy right now."

Abraham would somehow have to come to grips with the fact that not only was his sense of justice wrong, but so was his understanding of who God is. That would be just about the worst realization you could have as a human...a "sinners in the hands of an angry God"-type scenario.

Thankfully, "Yep," isn't God's answer. He lets Abraham in on a very interesting insight into his character as well as theology as a whole. God answers in verse 26, *"If I find at Sodom fifty righteous in the city, I will spare the whole place for their sake."* (Genesis 18:26, NIV)

Abraham just discovered that the doctrine of substitutionary atonement is a thing. Hmmm...so, the righteousness of some can atone for the unrighteousness of others. Interesting. Again, you can sense the wheels turning in Abraham's mind. "Interesting. So, God will spare bad people for the sake of good people. Hmmm... I wonder what God's number is. How many good save how many bad?" Abraham presses on. "Ok God, so how much goodness — or how many good people — does it take to prevent the smiting of an entire town? Is this a simple majority-type situation? 51%? If so, does a certain degree of righteousness matter? In other words, what if some of the righteous people are really great people and others are pretty good folks who attend church on Sundays and donate a little bit of money to charity?"

From there on out, Abraham tries to settle in on the level of righteousness needed to save the town. It's really not so different than the inner feeling we all have today about the town we care about most: the town of me. How much goodness in me will save me? 50 good deeds? What if I'm sort of an arrogant jerk a lot of the time, but I attend church on Sundays and give money to the poor? Is that enough to save me?

Abraham continues his theological discussion with God. 50 righteous people? What about 45? Yes, ok, how about 40? 30? 20? Then, in verse 32, he stops at 10...which is sort of weird because we can all see where this is going. I think he stops because ol' Abraham can see where this is going, too. Would God save the town for the sake of 1? Just one. I've heard lots of theories on why he stopped his haggling/questioning at 10 righteous people. Obviously, we don't know for sure, but here's the theory I tend to agree with: Abraham stopped because he realized that the fate of the town was going to rest on the number 1. In God's economics, it only takes one righteous to save all the unrighteous. In other words, Abraham realized that God's number was "one" and that the fate of Sodom might very well rest on one: his nephew, Lot. If Lot was righteous, the town would be saved. If not, it would be destroyed. Abraham didn't want to go there. He may have been thinking...what if I was in the city? Would I be considered righteous enough that God would save the city because of me? Again, this is all total supposition. But, perhaps these were a few thoughts that were running through Abraham's head.

Back to the logical conclusion. And it's ultimately a question of utmost importance for the whole of human existence. What if it wasn't just a sinful town but a sinful state and sinful country and sinful world? Would God spare a world of unrighteous people if there was only one righteous person in it? Would God save the world for just one? From this point on, the Bible answers that question unequivocally and beautifully. Yes, for the sake of one he will save it. Because of one he will save it. But, it has to be the right one. Truly righteous. Truly blameless. Truly perfect. And, just as he foreshadows four chapters later in Genesis 22, God will himself provide the perfect one...the perfect sacrifice.

So, the ultimate answer to that inner question we all have — "How much goodness in me will save me? How many good deeds must I do to outweigh the bad?" — is "None." With all the rhetoric about "doing enough good to convince St. Peter at the Pearly Gates to let us in"...that just isn't how things work, theologically. In fact, that's one of the core beliefs that sets Christianity apart from other religions. In Islam, your good deeds must outweigh your bad deeds. In Buddhism, you must essentially figure out some complex mental puzzle to discover "reality" and escape the confines of this world. In Christianity, the work of salvation doesn't depend on our physical, mental, or emotional ability...only our acceptance of a gift. We do not have the capacity to save ourselves by our own goodness. And, that's the best news ever; because it means the weight of our salvation is removed from us and placed somewhere else...on someone else. When judgment day comes — and the Bible promises us that it will come for all of us — we will not be rewarded with an eternity with our creator based on our own merit. God's number is, in fact, one. One righteous. One perfect sacrifice to redeem all of humanity. I'm not it. Neither are you. Jesus is. And, his work is done.

AMP up your study of Genesis 18

Apply — This week, have a real theological conversation with someone. Not an argument — a conversation. Ask a friend, family member, or coworker what they actually believe about salvation, goodness, and what happens when we die. Listen more than you talk. You might be surprised what comes up.

Meditate — Abraham's inner question was essentially: *how much goodness is enough?* Be honest — do you ever catch yourself keeping score? Feeling like you've been good enough lately to deserve God's favor, or bad enough to deserve his silence? What does it mean that God's number is one — and you're not it?

Pray — Thank God specifically that your salvation doesn't rest on your performance. Pray for someone in your life who is still trying to earn their way — carrying the weight of their own goodness as a ticket to God's grace. Ask God to show them the gift.

Next week: Genesis Chapter 19 — A History of Salt

Chapter Nineteen

Week Nineteen: A History of Salt

Genesis Chapter 19

Well, to say that Genesis 19 isn't my favorite chapter of the Bible would be putting it lightly. It begins with an entire town trying to gang rape some angels and ends with two daughters sleeping with their dad. The entire chapter makes me throw up in my mouth a little.

Rather than focusing on all the depravity, today I'm going to focus on 6 little words in this chapter that made no sense to me in the context of the story or in the context of reality. I mean, there are a lot of disturbing things in this chapter, but these six words seem so random and so bizarre that I couldn't help but focus on them. Here are the six words from verse 26: *"She became a pillar of salt."* What in the world is happening here? It seems like such a weird and random detail...especially in light of verses like Matthew 5:13...where it sounds like being the salt of the earth is a good thing. This is one of the many stories in the Bible that is so bizarre that it must be true. How could you even make something like this up? Why wasn't she just struck down by a hailstone or turned to dust or struck by lightning or swallowed up by the ground or something? Those things seem more like they were in God's Old Testament wheelhouse. Why salt? I know enough about the Bible to know that nothing is in it by accident. Every chapter has meaning. Every verse has meaning. So, there must be some reason for this. I've heard a lot of sermons in my life, and I've heard a few sermons on why Lot's wife turned into a pillar of salt; but I've never heard one on why salt, specifically. Perhaps there's a clue in the other mentions of salt in the Bible. So, I started there. Are you ready for a bit of a deep dive on the subject of salt? I didn't think so. Oh well. Here we go...

As it turns out, salt is mentioned throughout the Bible in a variety of contexts:

- Salt is mentioned in Leviticus and Ezekiel as a requirement to be part of the sacrifices.

- It was part of the incense in Exodus 30:35.

- It was a sign of a covenant of friendship in Numbers 18:19 and 2 Chronicles 13:5.

- It's a metaphorical name for desolate land in Psalm 107:34, Job 39:6, and Jeremiah 17:6.

- In Judges 9:45, Abimelek destroys a city, kills everyone, and scatters salt all over it.

- In Ezekiel 16:4, newborn babies were rubbed with salt.

- *"You are the salt of the earth. But if the salt loses its saltiness, how can it be made salty again? It is no longer good for anything, except to be thrown out and trampled underfoot."* (Matthew 5:13, NIV)

- *"Salt is good, but if it loses its saltiness, how can you make it salty again? Have salt among yourselves, and be at peace with each other."* (Mark 9:50, NIV)

- *"Let your conversation be always full of grace, seasoned with salt, so that you may know how to answer everyone."* (Colossians 4:6, NIV)

- Jews dip the Sabbath bread in salt. Bread is a symbol of food, a gift from God. Dipping it in salt preserves it. So, it's symbolic of preserving that gift.

So, salt means a lot of things. Being the nerd and slightly compulsive reader that I am, I had a brilliant thought: "I wonder if anyone has written a book about salt?" Believe it or not, the answer is yes. A guy by the name of Mark Kurlansky wrote the aptly titled *Salt: A World History*. I didn't see any way I could read a book about salt and keep my eyes open, so I downloaded it on Audible, listened to all 13 hours and 48 minutes of it, and took copious notes. That's right. 13 hours and 48 minutes about the history of salt. As it turns out, there's an awful lot to know about salt. Did you know that it has, according to Kurlansky, over 14,000 known uses? Among other fairly useless but otherwise interesting facts from his book:

- Adult humans contain about 250 grams of salt...or about 2–3 salt shakers' worth at any given time.

- Roman soldiers were sometimes paid in salt...hence the phrase "worth his salt." The Latin word for salt is *sal*, hence the term *salary*. The Latin word *sal* became the French word *sold* meaning "pay" and is the origin of the word *soldier*. The Romans salted their greens, hence the word *salad*.

- The French came up with over 265 different kinds of cheeses...primarily when trying to find ways to preserve milk in salt.

- One of Gandhi's acts that gained him a bunch of his followers was his defiance of the British salt laws and accompanying salt tax. This was a bit ironic since he, himself, abstained entirely from the substance.

- The US is the largest producer of salt. 8% of the salt we produce is used for food. 51% is for de-icing roads.

- The first patent issued in America was for a 10-year monopoly on saltworks.

- A number of the greatest public works ever conceived were motivated by the need to produce salt. Almost no place on earth is without salt. However, before modern geology discovered this, it was sought after, traded, and fought over; because it was not known that salt was everywhere.

- In 1670 in France, in an effort to lower suicide rates, those who died by suicide were ordered to be salted and put on public display.

- Chemically speaking, acids try to look for an electron that they are lacking and bases try to shed an extra electron. So, acids and bases have an affinity for each other. Like the rest of nature seemingly does, they long for completion. Together, acids and bases make a well-balanced compound: salt (sodium=base, chloride=acid). Salt is a microcosm for one of the oldest concepts in nature and the order of the universe as a whole — it's a yin/yang ionic compound.

- It was discovered that oil fields were often next to salt. The three most important oil fields in North America were found by drilling against geologists' advice but following knowledge of salt deposits.

There, do you feel more knowledgeable now? You're welcome. Do you now understand why Lot's wife turned into salt and not some other substance? Me either. But I have a few ideas.

First, let's go back to Kurlansky's book. I do recommend it, by the way. Great work, Mr. Kurlansky. He writes about the geography of the Dead Sea region:

"The oily water in the Dead Sea is bitter, as though it was cursed. ... The exact locations of Sodom and Gomorrah are unknown, but its residents are thought to have been salt workers and the towns are believed to have been located in the southern Dead Sea region. Since Genesis states that God annihilated all vegetation at the once-fertile spot, this barren, rocky area fits the description. But this area also has a mountain — more like a long jagged ridge — called Mount Sodom,

of almost pure salt carved by the elements into gothic pinnacles. According to the Book of Genesis, Abraham's nephew, Lot, lived in Sodom and was spared when God destroyed the town, but Lot's wife, who looked back at the destruction, was turned into salt. As columns break away from Mount Sodom, they are identified for tourists as Lot's wife. Unfortunately, they are unstable formations. The last Lot's wife collapsed several years ago, and the current one, featured in postcards and on guided tours, will go very soon, according to geologists." — Mark Kurlansky, *Salt: A World History*

Now, let's go back to the Bible. Salt is the symbol of the eternal nature of God's covenant with Israel. *"It is a covenant of salt forever before the Lord."* (Numbers 18:19, NIV) *"Don't you know that the Lord, the God of Israel, has given the kingship of Israel to David and his descendants forever by a covenant of salt?"* (2 Chronicles 13:5, NIV)

All that said, what's the answer? Why did Lot's wife become a pillar of salt? Here's what I think. And, I should note that this is speculation...because the Bible doesn't give an explanation.

As with many things in the Bible, I think there are a few layers of meaning here.

First, I think it's somewhat covenant-related. There's a pattern developing in Genesis. As you may recall, there's a covenant in chapter 15. Then, in chapter 16, Abram and Sarai try to take matters into their own hands rather than waiting on God's timing. Then, in chapter 17, there's another covenant discussion. In chapter 18, Sarah laughs at the fulfillment of the covenant...trivializing it. Then, here in chapter 19, we see a sign of a covenant...salt. It was a physical symbol that in her heart, Lot's wife's covenant was with Sodom. If Kurlansky is right, there's a decent chance she had become a salt worker like many if not most of the town's other inhabitants. If that was the case — and again, I'd like to emphasize that this is speculation — she may have become the thing she idolized. If that's the case, the lesson is this: once you have become a Christian, it can become incredibly tempting to go back to life as it was. It's like an alcoholic saying that he's strong enough to just have a drink here and there. But, he's not. We're not. Whatever we look back to will inevitably consume us. We won't master it. It will master us. Just as in the lesson Joseph taught us with Potiphar's wife. Sometimes the best answer isn't rationalization. It isn't trying to have a calm conversation with a seductress. The best answer is to flee. To run. And to never look back. Otherwise, you risk becoming consumed by the idols of your past. Everyone becomes consumed by something. We all have that thing we look to or run to in times of great stress. These days, it isn't salt mines. It's alcohol or caffeine or rage or social media or sugar or fill-in-the-blank. And, I think there are still times where God wants us to flee the comfortable and never look back...or risk becoming the thing we worship.

I'll leave you with this from Tim Keller's *King's Cross*:

"If you say, 'I'll obey you, Jesus, if my career thrives, if my health is good, if my family is together,' then the thing that's on the other side of that if is your real master, your real goal. But Jesus will not be a means to an end; he will not be used. If he calls you to follow him, he must be the goal." — Tim Keller, *King's Cross*

AMP up your study of Genesis 19

Apply — Identify the thing you most naturally run to in times of great stress — not the thing you know you *should* run to, but the thing you actually do. Name it honestly. Then, this week, the next time stress hits, make a deliberate choice to run toward God first before running to your default.

Meditate — Lot's wife was free. She was literally walking away from destruction. And she looked back. What is the Sodom in your own life that you keep glancing back at — the thing God has already delivered you from that still has a hold on your gaze? What would it look like to never look back at it again?

Pray — Pray the prayer of Psalm 119:37 this week: *"Turn my eyes away from worthless things; preserve my life according to your word."* Pray it every morning. Write it on a sticky note. Let it become your prayer for the week.

Next week: Genesis Chapter 20 — Abraham and Abimelech

Chapter Twenty

Week Twenty: A Person God Uses

Genesis Chapter 20

"*And Abraham said of Sarah his wife, 'She is my sister.' And Abimelech king of Gerar sent and took Sarah. But God came to Abimelech in a dream by night and said to him, 'Behold, you are a dead man because of the woman whom you have taken, for she is a man's wife.'*" (Genesis 20:2–3, ESV)

For the most part, the quote-unquote "heroes of the Bible" aren't often hero-like. They're sometimes scared, sometimes cowardly, sometimes unfaithful, sometimes overly zealous, sometimes prone to amazing levels of blithering idiocy. And, every single one of them gives me hope for my future.

Here we have Abraham. This is a guy who God spoke to directly. Not only that, but he had seen firsthand the powerful justice of God...and not like many decades before. Like, the previous chapter before. Also, it was only two chapters before this in which God promised him a son. In fact, in Genesis 18:10, God promised that approximately one year from then He would return and Sarah would have a son. Did Abraham march forward in faith, comfort, obedience, and overwhelming joy for the forthcoming year? No. He feared for his life to the point that he lied about his wife being his sister. Then, Abimelech took her. Did

Abraham speak up and try to prevent his wife from being taken away? Nope. Well, at least the Bible doesn't mention it if he did. He seemingly just let her go. Reminder: this is the same guy who, back in Genesis 14, courageously took 318 men and chased after and defeated an army who had taken his nephew, Lot. So, if I'm reading this correctly...Abraham's nephew gets taken and he boldly chases down an army to free him. His wife gets taken and he's like, "Welp, that's unfortunate. Hope I see her again someday."

And, this guy is the patriarch of patriarchs.

Here's my takeaway from this. 1) It is human nature to doubt the promises of God. Time and time again in the Bible you see regular, ordinary people who God uses in spite of their monumental mess-ups. 2) God is faithful with his end of the deal. He doesn't say, "Well, I told you Sarah would have a baby in a year; but that deal is off now. I'll go find someone else to be the patriarch of patriarchs who has more faith in me." No, God follows through. He tells his story through the faithful and the faithless. The strong and the weak. The child and the orphan. The captive and the free. Jews, Egyptians, Romans, Greeks. Women and men. Children and elderly. Blind and lame. On that note, if we ever doubt the beauty of diversity, we need only look at the people God chose to tell his story through. God tells his perfect story through imperfect people. To me, that's the subtle message here. This isn't the story of Abraham learning some lessons and becoming a hero for the ages that we should all model our lives after. This is the story of God's perfect grace, mercy, peace, hope, and love as told through a doubting little human. And, if God can tell his story so powerfully through a guy like Abraham, perhaps he can tell a pretty powerful story with me as well. Perhaps he can tell a pretty powerful story with you, too. Did you mess up monumentally this week? I bet you didn't willingly let your wife be trafficked to a foreign land. Give yourself some grace. It isn't the end of your story. It might just be the beginning.

AMP up your study of Genesis 20

Apply — Write down one specific way you have doubted God's promises in the last month. Then write down one specific way God has been faithful despite that doubt. Keep both lists and let the second one inform how you approach the first.

Meditate — Abraham courageously rescued his nephew but passively let his wife be taken. We all have inconsistencies like this — areas where we're bold for God and areas where fear takes over completely. Where are yours? What does your particular brand of inconsistency reveal about what you most deeply fear?

Pray — Thank God that he tells his perfect story through imperfect people. Pray for the grace to stop disqualifying yourself from being used by God because of your failures. Ask him to use your mess as part of his message.

Next week: Genesis Chapter 21 — Isaac Is Born

Chapter Twenty-One

Week Twenty-One: "Yeah, Right." to "Wow, Right?"

Genesis Chapter 21

In Genesis 21, we have the birth of Isaac and the protection of Hagar and Ishmael. The meaning of the name Isaac strikes me, so that's where we begin this week.

"He laughs." There's quite a story wrapped up in that name.

You may remember these verses from Genesis 18:

"The Lord said, 'I will surely return to you about this time next year, and Sarah your wife shall have a son.' And Sarah was listening at the tent door behind him. Now Abraham and Sarah were old, advanced in years. The way of women had ceased to be with Sarah. So Sarah laughed to herself, saying, 'After I am worn out, and my lord is old, shall I have pleasure?' The Lord said to Abraham, 'Why did Sarah laugh and say, "Shall I indeed bear a child, now that I am old?" Is anything too hard for the Lord? At the appointed time I will return to you, about this time next year, and Sarah shall have a son.' But Sarah denied it, saying, 'I did not

laugh,' for she was afraid. He said, 'No, but you did laugh.'" (Genesis 18:10–15, ESV)

Now, in chapter 21, verse 6, we read this: *"And Sarah said, 'God has made laughter for me; everyone who hears will laugh over me.' And she said, 'Who would have said to Abraham that Sarah would nurse children? Yet I have borne him a son in his old age.'"* (Genesis 21:6–7, ESV)

God turned Sarah's laughter of disbelief into laughter of resolve and joy. In fact, her personal laughter of disbelief turned into corporate laughter of resolve and joy. Her [laughter] "Yeah, right." turned into everyone's [laughter] "Wow, right?" That's a powerful story. And, that is a pretty good name for a patriarch of the Israelites.

The same could be said for us. God is really good at turning our laughing "Yeah, right." into resolved laughter of "Wow, right?" — to the point that everyone around us joins in the laughter of "Wow, right?" I can think of a few examples. I've known people battling addiction who, if God himself had shown up and said, "The desire to inject this substance will be gone from your life. You'll have a job you love, a family who loves you, and people who want to be like you," their response would have been [laughter] "Yeah, right." Then, when it happens, they can't respond any other way than [laughter] "Wow, right?" The response is the same for everyone who knows their story. [laughter] "Wow, right?" I've known parents who, if you'd told them their wayward child would someday be a remarkable leader, they would've responded exactly like Sarah. The [laughter] "Yeah, right." Then, Jesus moves. And everyone surrounding that kid who knows his or her story joins the parents in the [laughter] "Wow, right?"

Ok, there's a lot going on in this chapter, so let's look at another theological concept here. It's the concept of the least will become the greatest. Older will serve the younger. This is a pattern that will be repeated throughout the Bible.

Moses. A stutterer leads the negotiation talks with Pharaoh.

David. The youngest son becomes the king.

Gideon. The weakest member of the weakest tribe leads God's army.

Jacob. The younger deceiver brother becomes the patriarch of the nation of Israel.

Joseph. The younger brother becomes the savior.

Ehud. A left-handed Benjamite — son of the right — saves the nation.

A prostitute saves the spies of God.

Paul. A mass-murderer of Christians becomes the author of much of the New Testament.

Most importantly, the son of a teenage mom and carpenter dad from po-dunkville, Israel proves himself to be the savior of the world.

I can't leave this chapter without talking about verse 13, because that's where I — and most of you, I imagine — feel as though I enter the story of the Bible. I'm not a Jew. I'm a Gentile. *And I will make a nation of the son of the slave woman also, because he is your offspring.* As much as I want to fashion myself as one of the heroes of the Bible sometimes, Ishmael is closer to my heritage. To be fair, I haven't ever done a deep dive into genealogy to know for sure whether I'm ultimately from the line of Isaac or the line of Ishmael or the line of some pagan nation or something. Probably the latter. Anyhow, I more closely relate to the outcast son of a slave woman than the chosen line of Isaac.

As God has a pattern of doing throughout the Bible, God meets Hagar at a well. In fact, it appears before her eyes. Fast forward. Keeping with the Bible's trend of the Old Testament being physical representations of spiritual realities, we again see God meet a woman at a well in the New Testament. She is also a slave woman, though she is slave to the sin of adultery rather than a person. No doubt Jesus, as he met this slave woman at a well in the New Testament, recounted this moment — this encounter with Hagar thousands of years prior in the Old Testament. His words are the same. Instead of a physical well manifesting, Jesus completes the picture that has waited thousands of years. It's almost as if he's saying, "That water that I showed Hagar...that drink I gave Ishmael? I am that drink. I am that water. I am the way, the truth, and the life for you personally and for any other people living a life in bondage. There is hope. And hope is here."

And, that's the story of Genesis 21. Hope? A future? [laughter] Yeah, right. I'm doomed to die in slavery. There's no path forward for me. There's no hope. There's no life. A way out? [laughter] Yeah, right.

Enter Jesus. [laughter] I am the way, the truth, and the life. I have water. I have hope. I have freedom. Wow, right?

Here's my takeaway this week. Think about a seemingly impossible, unresolvable frustration in your life right now. We all have them. Perhaps it's a broken relationship. Perhaps it's an addiction. Perhaps it's a job situation. Perhaps it's a budget situation. What is something in your life for which, if someone told you it could be resolved, you would laugh, "Yeah, right!"? Take time this week to pray through that thing. Pray specifically that God turns the "Yeah, right!" into a testimony of "Wow, right?"

AMP up your study of Genesis 21

Apply — Find someone whose story has gone from "Yeah, right." to "Wow, right?" — someone whose life God has turned around in a way that seemed impossible. Reach out to them this week and tell them their story has encouraged you. Let them know their testimony matters.

Meditate — The pattern of the least becoming the greatest runs all the way through Scripture. Moses the stutterer. David the youngest. Paul the murderer. Where do you see yourself on that list? What is the thing about you that seems like a disqualifier that God might actually want to use?

Pray — Name your "Yeah, right." out loud to God this week. The thing that feels impossible, unresolvable, too far gone. Pray it specifically. Then pray for the faith to leave room for a "Wow, right?" — even if you can't see how it gets there from here.

Next week: Genesis Chapter 22 — Isaac on the Altar

Chapter Twenty-Two

Week Twenty-Two: Sacrifice and Salvation

Genesis Chapter 22

Well, we've made it to yet another supremely uncomfortable chapter in the Bible. The God of the universe, who created man in his image and loves him, promises a child to a barren woman. He makes good on that promise. Then, the very next chapter, God commands the father — to whom he made said promise — to kill his son...the son of the promise.

By any rational standard — emotionally, theologically, etc. — at first glance, this chapter makes no sense. Absolutely no sense. So, what is happening here?

Fortunately, God paints the picture immediately.

"Take your son, your only son Isaac, whom you love, and go to the land of Moriah." (Genesis 22:2, ESV)

"And Abraham took the wood of the burnt offering and laid it on Isaac his son." (Genesis 22:6, ESV)

Fast forward a few thousand years. We see the exact same image again.

"And behold, a voice from heaven said, 'This is my beloved Son, with whom I am well pleased.'" (Matthew 3:17, NIV — echoed in Mark 1:11 and Luke 3:22)

"Carrying his own cross, he went out to the place of the Skull (which in Aramaic is called Golgotha)." (John 19:17, NIV)

"'The fire and wood are here,' Isaac said, 'but where is the lamb for the burnt offering?' Abraham answered, 'God himself will provide the lamb for the burnt offering, my son.'" (Genesis 22:7–8, NIV)

"Look, the Lamb of God, who takes away the sin of the world!" (John 1:29, NIV)

As soon as God held back the hand of Abraham, he committed to the death of his own son, Jesus.

That's the picture he's trying to paint. A God of the universe who created Abraham and Isaac knew what the response of Abraham would be. This wasn't a situation where God was sitting up in Heaven nervously waiting to see what Abraham would choose. This wasn't a test so much as it was an illustration. For the blessing to come, ultimate sacrifice must be made. Sin must be atoned for. Debt must be paid. The problem of evil must be resolved. Accounts must be reconciled. And, God will provide the lamb. And, humans will kill him with their hands. And all of humanity will feel the same relief and joy Abraham felt as he experienced the grace of a God who atoned for his sins for him.

Holding Abraham's hand back from his son meant releasing God's hand on his own son. Sparing Isaac meant condemning Jesus.

Killing Isaac would have killed the line. It would have put a nail in the genealogy of Jesus. It would have destroyed the promise. In other words, killing Isaac would have doomed humanity, spared Jesus, and killed the promise. Sparing Isaac saves humanity, kills Jesus, and fulfills the promise.

That's the illustration.

I've been watching old seasons of the TV show *Alone*. If you haven't seen the show, here's the premise: 10 contestants are dropped off in a remote location of the world with limited supplies and no camera crew. Whoever survives on their own the longest wins. One thing that has struck me is the deep need for humanity to do something with the wrongness inside of them...the sin in their lives. It seems that every contestant who remains past the first few days, regardless of their religion, wrestles with their inner demons. Left alone with their thoughts long enough, they feel a need to repent or make right the wrong in their lives. They feel a need to do something with that remorse. They feel like they have a debt that needs to be paid. I think that is something that is fundamental to humanity. We all have some sense of wrong and right. And, we all have some deep inner need to reconcile the badness in us.

To me, that's the power of Genesis 22. It reaches into that deep need and says, "You're right." There is a need to reconcile that. And, the price is high. In fact it's higher than you can imagine. Imagine a son whom you've not only hoped for for decades, but built a relationship with for years after the rejoicing of his unlikely birth. Imagine that the blood of something that pure and good — a source of total joy in your life — must be sacrificed to make things right. In other words, something must die so that you might live. And you know what, all of life reiterates this. That's pretty much how food works, right? Whether carnivore or vegetarian, every time we eat we are reminded that some animal or plant must die so that we might live. In fact, often times the more pure the thing that dies, the more abundant the life it gives. It's as if God built the illustration into creation and nature itself.

To me, that's Genesis 22 in a nutshell. God is showing Abraham that the pathway to life is via the death of the purest, most beautiful thing. And, he's doing it in a way Abraham will never forget — in a way no one will ever forget: telling him to lay his beloved son upon some wood and sacrifice him.

AMP up your study of Genesis 22

Apply — Watch an episode or two of *Alone* this week — or any show that puts people in true solitude — and pay attention to how the contestants wrestle with their inner lives when there are no distractions. Use it as a mirror. What would you wrestle with if left alone with your thoughts for a week?

Meditate — Sparing Isaac meant condemning Jesus. Sit with that equation for a moment. God held back Abraham's hand and released his own. What does it mean to you personally that God made that trade — not in theory, but for you specifically?

Pray — Pray through the parallel passages this week: Genesis 22:7–8 and John 1:29. Ask God to make the connection between Abraham's altar and the cross feel real and personal to you — not just theological, but deeply human. Thank him for providing the lamb.

Next week: Genesis Chapter 23 — The Promised Land

Chapter Twenty-Three

Week Twenty-Three: The Promised Land

Genesis Chapter 23

Here we find the story of Abraham purchasing the only land he would ever own in the land that was promised to him. The death of his wife compelled him to purchase this plot. A couple of takeaways here:

First, it was important that this land was bought with a price. This conveyed legal title to Abraham in perpetuity. This is interesting, because Abraham was an immigrant who had been nomadically living in this area for some 62 years.

Let's look at this place. Hebron.

This is the area that Moses would send the spies — including Joshua and Caleb — into to check out the land (Numbers 13). Joshua eventually conquers it in Joshua 10, gives it to Caleb in Joshua 14, allots it to Caleb's tribe of Judah in Joshua 21, and specifically allots the city of Hebron to the Levites. We see Hebron again in 2 Samuel 2 when David is anointed king there. It becomes the capital city for King David's kingdom. So, Hebron's geography carries a ton of significance. In addition to being the location of the tomb of the patriarchs, it's the key city of the tribe of Judah — out of which the savior of the world would come — and the city of priests and kings. So, it's a geographical triumvirate of allusions to Christ. The name Hebron itself means "joining" or "alliance" — as in God joining man, or God's alliance with man. Jews inhabited Hebron until 1100 when expelled by Crusaders, reestablished a presence a hundred or so years later, and remained there until 1929 when they fled from Muslim persecution. Then, following the Six-Day War in 1967, the Jewish community was re-established there. The city has been a hotbed for violence throughout history. A church was built over the tomb of the patriarchs, remade into a mosque, then a church again, a couple of times.[1] The location is still a source of much fighting and conflict to this day.

It is interesting that this first relatively tiny plot of land in the so-called promised land was not given to Abraham but had to be purchased by him. And, it was purchased not for living, but for burying the dead. Abraham, Isaac, Jacob, Rebekah, and Leah would later join Sarah here. According to Jewish tradition, Adam and Eve are also buried here.[2]

When I think through the general theme of the Old Testament — physical realities representing spiritual truths — what is God trying to show us here?

For one, it's significant that the first foray into receiving the promised land of God was a burying of the dead. In fact, it was purchasing the place where Abraham would one day be buried as well. For Sarah, this would be her first permanent residence in the promised land: in her own grave. For me, that's the picture here. Our entrance into the promised land starts with our burial. Death is the first step to permanent residence in the land God has promised us: a life infused with peace and joy. It is important to note that a life of peace and joy does not equate to a life of worldly prosperity or power or health or success...but a life of peace and joy no matter what life brings. In America, we've mostly been taught that permanent residence in a life of peace and joy begins with our success...our triumph. Modernity teaches us that a life of peace and joy begins with our personal conquering of demons or mastering some skill or building a perfect relationship. But, the Bible teaches something very different. It teaches a counterintuitive idea: that residence in a life of peace and joy begins not with our achievement, but with a death. A death to our self. A death to the idea that we can fix things on our own. And in that death, we find life. We find the promised land.

---

¹ Wikipedia, "History of the Jews in Hebron," en.wikipedia.org. ² Hebron.org.il, "Adam and Eve in Hebron," hebron.org.il.

AMP up your study of Genesis 23

Apply — Identify one area of your life where you are still waiting for God to simply *give* you something — a relationship, an opportunity, a breakthrough — rather than being willing to pay a price for it. What would it look like to stop waiting passively and take one faithful step toward it this week, even if that step costs you something?

Meditate — Sarah's first permanent address in the promised land was her grave. The entrance to life is through death — to self, to control, to the idea that we can fix things on our own. Where in your life are you still trying to earn or achieve your way into peace rather than dying to it? What does it actually mean for you to die to self in a practical, daily sense?

Pray — Ask God to show you what needs to be buried in your life so that something new can grow. Pray for the courage to let it die — the pride, the control, the self-sufficiency — and trust that the promised land is on the other side of that burial, not before it.

Next week: Genesis Chapter 24 — Isaac and Rebekah

Chapter Twenty-Four

Week Twenty-Four: God Listens

Genesis Chapter 24

One of the patterns worth noting as we move through Genesis is this: many significant events in the Bible take place at water wells. I once heard a preacher say that anytime you see a well in the Bible, pay close attention to what God is trying to say there. So, I did that here. Genesis 24 is the story of Isaac's wife being found at a well.

Before we get to the well, it is worth noting that one of the first recorded prayers in the Bible is found in verse 12 of this chapter. In it, the servant asks for a sign from God. Also worth noting: here are a few other examples of prayers where people asked God to give them a sign — or God told someone to ask for a sign: Judges 6:17, Isaiah 38:22, Isaiah 7:11. In this case in Genesis 24, the servant's prayer is met with an immediate answer. I love those prayers, by the way. And, I've absolutely had that happen — both in trivial matters and not-so-trivial ones. Please, God, let me find my keys. Boom. Keys. Please, God, give me the opportunity to talk to my friend about x situation that just happened. Boom. Phone call from friend.

For me, the message here is to be real with God. If you're having doubts, express them. You can't hide them from God anyway, so you might as well be real about it.

Now, we're at the well.

Isaac's servant has prayed for a sign: specifically to make the wife-hunting expedition easier on him.

"May it be that when I say to a young woman, 'Please let down your jar that I may have a drink,' and she says, 'Drink, and I'll water your camels too' — let her be the one you have chosen for your servant Isaac." (Genesis 24:14, NIV)

And, that's exactly what Rebekah says and does. As you may or may not be aware, this was no small ask. First, according to Google, camels drink up to 20 gallons at a time. Verse 10 tells us that Isaac's servant had 10 camels with him. Simple math: Rebekah was committing to drawing as many as 200 gallons of water out of a well. And, we know she was only carrying one jar. That's an absurd amount of labor.

"After she had given him a drink, she said, 'I'll draw water for your camels too, until they have had enough to drink.' So she quickly emptied her jar into the trough, ran back to the well to draw more water, and drew enough for all his camels. Without saying a word, the man watched her closely to learn whether or not the Lord had made his journey successful. When the camels had finished drinking, the man took out a gold nose ring weighing a beka and two gold bracelets weighing ten shekels. Then he asked, 'Whose daughter are you? Please tell me, is there room in your father's house for us to spend the night?'" (Genesis 24:19–23, NIV)

Side note: if you've ever drawn even one bucket of water out of an old well via an old rope, you know that this is no small task. I had the privilege of doing exactly that on one of our trips to Kenya. There's a bit of a technique to drawing water out of a well; and, even with the proper technique, it wore me out. But, I digress. This poor girl makes who knows how many trips to the well and back. Did Isaac's servant make small talk or offer to help or encourage her with "thank you"s? No — verse 21 tells us that he watches her every move in silence like a creeper, not helping at all...or offering to help at all.

All that said, what's my takeaway from Genesis 24?

First, we have yet another example of God showing up in the midst of action. I'll admit that I don't always have a bias toward action. My wife has more of a ready, fire, aim mentality whereas I'm more ready, aim, aim, aim, aim, aim, second guess, aim, aim, maybe fire if my spreadsheet tells me my chances of success are statistically worthwhile. Much of the time in the Bible when God encounters people, God does so as they're working or doing something. On a journey. On the threshing floor. Working at their job. Drawing water from a well. Serving people. Etc. Personally, this was a reminder to be praying as I'm acting...and acting while praying.

Second, let's go back to the first recorded prayer in the Bible. Theologically speaking, it's fascinating to me that a human can throw up a request for a specific sign and God honor that request. Call me crazy, but I believe that to be true still.

I've had the opportunity to speak to a few groups about my son's very rare medical condition and how God is working in the midst of it. One question I've asked the groups is this: have you ever misplaced your keys or wallet or document or something and thrown a quick prayer up to God — "Please help me find my keys or phone or whatever?" — and then, miraculously, found whatever item? And then pretty quickly thereafter, discounted it as luck or "well, of course it was in the last place I looked..." or something? When I asked for a show of hands, do you know how many hands went up? Almost every single one.

I don't know where you're at in this whole "Where do I fit in the cosmos? ... Is there a higher power? ... How does this all work?" thing; but, here's where I'm at: I believe there is a very real God who packed everything we need to know about our purpose here into the written scriptures of the Bible and then personified those words in the form of Jesus Christ. And, I believe that same creator God still interacts with us little humans today in mysterious ways — from helping us find lost keys to bringing people back from the dead to finding a wife for a guy at a well. And, for some mysterious reason, the same God of the universe places a high value on humans conversing with him.

So, that's my takeaway from Genesis 24: God listens. I just need to remember to start the conversation more often.

AMP up your study of Genesis 24

Apply — This week, pray specifically and concretely about something — not just a vague "be with me today" prayer, but a specific request with a specific outcome. Then pay attention. Write down what happens. Don't talk yourself out of it if God shows up.

Meditate — The servant prayed while he was acting — on a journey, in the middle of his work. How often do you pray while you're moving versus only when you're still? What would it look like to weave conversation with God into the ordinary motion of your day?

Pray — Pray the servant's prayer this week in your own words: ask God for a specific sign or confirmation about something you've been uncertain about. Be honest with him about your doubts. Then watch closely — like the servant at the well — without saying a word.

Next week: Genesis Chapter 25 — Jacob and Esau

Chapter Twenty-Five

Week Twenty-Five: Jacob and Esau

Genesis Chapter 25

In Genesis 25, we find the story of the death of Abraham as well as the birth of Jacob and Esau.

Keeping with my theme of trying to read through these Genesis chapters as if I'd never read them before, nothing really stood out to me until I re-read the last part of the chapter: the part about Jacob and Esau. For starters, we see yet another miraculous birth from a barren woman. And, there's a pretty big contrast between how Abraham handled he and his wife's infertility and how Isaac and Rebekah handled theirs. Abraham and Sarah tried to force God's promise to happen via sex with a servant girl. Isaac prayed. Maybe he'd learned a lesson from his father? Who knows? That's a pretty easy lesson to follow: if you ever find yourself presented with the options of A) praying; or, B) having sex with your wife's maidservant, you should choose option A.

Anyhow, that's probably important to note, but here's my main takeaway from Genesis 25: it comes from the famous story of Esau selling his birthright for a bowl of soup. First, a quick rehash:

Esau returns home from a hunting trip. Apparently, it's been a long and challenging trip because he is absolutely exhausted. He finds Jacob cooking up some stew. Esau, acting like a stereotypical eldest child, demands that Jacob give him some of the stew. Jacob's response: "Sure. No problem. I just need your birthright." Esau is taken aback but is like, "Dude, I'm about to die anyway from exhaustion and starvation if I don't get some food in me. That birthright doesn't do me much good if I'm dead. Sure. Take it." Jacob says, "Ok. By pure coincidence, I happen to have the contract drawn up and a notary present. Just initial here, here, here, and here; and, sign and date at the bottom." Esau signs, eats, drinks, and walks away...probably with a bit of a feeling of, "I feel like I might have overreacted a bit there..."

Ok so, that wasn't exactly how the story went down, but you get the gist of it.

At its core, this is a lesson on impulsivity. We humans have a bad habit of trading what we want most for what we want now. Esau is saying to God and to everyone else: I don't need the inheritance. I can attain everything myself. I can find my own joy. I can find my own fortune. I can find my own peace. Bad impulse.

We've seen quite the pattern of this issue so far, and we're barely halfway through the first book of the Bible.

Adam takes the fruit from Eve. "I don't need God. I'd feel complete if I had the knowledge of good and evil." We do the same thing today, by the way. We don't need God. We've got knowledge. We've got TED Talks and Google and YouTube — ironically, all on an iPhone...that happens to have a picture of a piece of fruit with a bite out of it on the back. Humanity really hasn't progressed all that much in all these years. Adam tries to gain satisfaction in his life with knowledge by way of a bite of fruit. Bad impulse.

Cain tries to satisfy his jealousy with murder. He kills Abel in Genesis 4. He doesn't need God. He thought he would feel better and feel a sense of justice if he followed his inner impulse and killed Abel. Bad impulse.

We've already talked about Abraham. Abraham didn't like God's timing. He impulsively took the maidservant from Sarah in an effort to create his family his way rather than God's. Bad impulse.

Tower of Babel. It's a whole group of people saying, "We don't need God. If we can just build this tower, we would feel complete and successful." Bad impulse.

Now, we come to Esau. Esau trading his birthright for stew is a continuation of the narrative of the perils of impulsivity. Adam sold out for knowledge. Cain sold out for vengeance. Abraham sold out for sex. Humanity sold out for pride and power. And Esau sold out for soup.

Of course, we all want wisdom, knowledge, success, and blessing. But, we're impulsive. We continually try to do it our way rather than God's.

Enter Jesus.

"Jesus, full of the Holy Spirit, left the Jordan and was led by the Spirit into the wilderness, where for forty days he was tempted by the devil. He ate nothing during those days, and at the end of them he was hungry. The devil said to him, 'If you are the Son of God, tell this stone to become bread.' Jesus answered, 'It is written: Man shall not live on bread alone.'" (Luke 4:1–4, NIV)

And with that, Jesus sets the example for how to handle impulsivity.

He's essentially saying, "This ends here. Impulsivity ends here. Selling out and selling short ends here. Satan's stranglehold over humanity and that thing he does where he convinces people that immediate things are better than God's eternal blessing...it's over. It's finished. Man doesn't live by impulsivity or what feels good alone, but on the word of God."

One more note. Later on, in the book of Luke, we see another story of impulsivity. It's in Luke 15:11–32. It's the story of the prodigal son. The story of the prodigal son almost seems to be a continuation of Esau's story. This is where impulsivity leads — where it leads when we "follow our heart" and do what "feels right" or "what is right in our own eyes"...when we follow our desires rather than allowing the Bible to guide us. We give up inheritance for living on impulse now. Fortunately, forgiveness waits in the end. What happens when we sell out for knowledge or vengeance or sex or pride or power or soup? What happens when we realize our mistake, when we feel the emptiness, when we feel utterly helpless, when we feel the crushing weight of our own impulsive bad choices, when we run back home unworthy of forgiveness but desperately needing it? What do we get? Rejected? Turned away? A bill to be paid? A lecture? No. We get a loving embrace. Forgiveness. Celebration. Redemption. Grace. Not because we deserve it but because Jesus bought it. Today, we get grace when we sell out for soup. All we have to do is run home and ask.

AMP up your study of Genesis 25

Apply — Identify your "soup" — the thing you are most tempted to trade your long-term inheritance for in moments of weakness. Write it down. Then write down what you are actually giving up when you reach for it. Keep that list somewhere visible this week as a reminder of what's really at stake.

Meditate — The pattern of impulsivity runs from Adam all the way to Esau without a break: knowledge, vengeance, sex, pride, power, soup. Where does your personal version of this pattern show up most consistently? What does your particular flavor of "bad impulse" reveal about what you're ultimately hungry for?

Pray — Pray the prayer of Luke 4 over your life this week. Ask God to meet you in your wilderness — the place where you're hungry and the temptation to grab something now is loudest. Ask him to give you the strength to say, "Man shall not live on bread alone," and mean it.

Next week: Genesis Chapter 26 — Isaac and Abimelech

Chapter Twenty-Six

Week Twenty-Six: The God of Your Father

Genesis Chapter 26

Here in Genesis 26, we find a couple of interesting parallels.

First, we find Isaac in a land of famine meeting Abimelech. Later, Isaac refers to his wife as his sister.

His father, Abraham, dealt with famine back in Genesis 12:10 and met Abimelech — probably a different Abimelech, but still — in chapter 20. Abraham also referred to his wife as his sister. Twice.

Anytime we see similar stories in the Bible, there's usually a deeper message there. It's almost as if God uses repetition to shine a spotlight on particular biblical stories. There are a ton of parallel stories in the Bible. For example, we have Isaac born from a barren woman, along with Jacob and Samson and Jesus born from barren women. We have the story of depravity in Sodom and Gomorrah and an eerily similar story at the end of the book of Judges in Gibeah. The prophet Jonah falls asleep on a boat only to be roused awake by panicked passengers in the Old Testament; and, Jesus falls asleep on a boat only to be roused awake by panicked passengers in the New Testament. The list goes on and on. There's immense depth to each of those stories. So, what point is God trying to get across here in the parallel stories of Genesis 20 and 26?

You probably have your own takeaways from Genesis 26. Here are mine.

First — and this is more of a side note than a takeaway, I suppose — we have a situation here where an immoral believer is called out by a moral unbeliever. I can think of a few Christians who need to hear that this happens sometimes. Just because we believe what is right doesn't mean that we are always right.

What caught me this week was verse 24: *"I am the God of your father Abraham."* (NIV)

While I don't think this was the point of this verse, I very much took this as a parenting challenge. What if God showed up to one of my kids and said, "I am the God of your father Josh."

How much would my kids know about God based on my life and words alone? What feelings would that spark in them?

What if Isaac's response would've been, "You'll have to tell me about you, God, because my dad never did." Or, "If you're the God of my father Abraham, I'd like to find a different God."

Think about this statement from your kids' perspective.

Actually, I'll extend the same challenge to you that I gave myself: if someone approached your kids and said to them, "Describe the God of your father and mother," — based on the habits of your day-to-day life, how would your kids describe the God you serve? How would they describe where you spend your time, energy, and resources? Would your kids say things like, "He prayed before dinner. We showed up at church a lot. We gave money to some places." Would they say something like, "My dad believed in the importance of following God, but he was much more passionate about the Dallas Cowboys or the republicans or the democrats or work or golf." Or, would they say things like, "I saw lives changed around my family. I saw my dad pray and his Bible open throughout my life. I saw him peaceful when he shouldn't have been. I saw him dole out grace and mercy with his time, money, and talent. I saw him work to have a relationship with God rather than offering up a bunch of impersonal transactions to some theoretical deity in the sky." I'd want them to say things more like that.

And, that is my takeaway this week: what habits can I begin forming today to improve my kids' impression of the God I serve? I'd encourage you to think through the same question.

AMP up your study of Genesis 26

Apply — Ask one of your kids — or a young person close to you — this week: "What do you think God is like?" Don't coach them. Just listen. Their answer will tell you a lot about what they've observed in your life. Then ask yourself what you want to do about it.

Meditate — "I am the God of your father Abraham." What would it mean for God to introduce himself to the next generation as the God of your household? What would he be able to point to as evidence? What habits, rhythms, or moments in your home reflect the character of the God you say you serve?

Pray — Pray specifically for the spiritual legacy you are leaving. Ask God to show you one concrete habit — not a program or a checklist, but a living, breathing, daily thing — that would make the next generation more likely to say, "I know that God. I've seen him at work."

Next week: Genesis Chapter 27 — Jacob Steals the Blessing

Chapter Twenty-Seven

Week Twenty-Seven: Jacob Steals the Blessing

Genesis Chapter 27

A couple of chapters ago in Genesis 25, we discussed Esau somewhat impulsively selling his birthright. Here in Genesis 27, he is tricked out of his blessing. Beginning in verse 19 we see Jacob steal Esau's blessing by pretending to be his stronger, hairy, outdoorsman, hunter older brother. You can tell that Isaac senses something is off. "How did you return so quickly?" "Um, come closer so I can make sure it's really you." "Hmmm...the voice seems wrong, but the arms feel right." "Are you really Esau?" "Um, yes, it's totally me, Esau." I imagine him saying "Esau" in a Batman-ish voice. When Isaac gets a whiff of the clothing, he takes that as confirmation. Then, he blesses him.

Here we see a continuation of a pattern throughout the Old Testament: God bypasses the firstborn to pass his inheritance and blessing on to the younger, rebellious, and often outright deceptive — as seen here — child. To me, that's the first thing I noticed here: God is painting a picture that is fulfilled in Christ — cursed firstborn, blessed younger. The other thing that hit me this week was the prevalence of this pattern in the Bible: God chooses to use a long line of messy people to bring blessing to the world. And, "messy" is putting it too lightly. These "heroes of the Bible" are like Jacob — deceivers and con artists, at best. They are prostitutes, murderers, adulterers, idolaters, and swindlers. If you were to Google "heroes of the Bible," you would find that these people broke every one of the ten commandments. Sometimes in a blaze of unholy glory. I think King David, "the man after God's own heart," broke like 5 out of 10 commandments in one fell swoop.

Now, it's hard for me to step back from my Christian background. It's hard for me to read the Bible in an unbiased way. I've been around it too long. But, wouldn't it make a lot more sense from a literary perspective to have the line of Jesus be full of kings, conquerors, and nobility rather than a bunch of sinful, horrendously broken people? I'm thinking David without the affairs and murder. Isaac without the "my wife's my sister" junk. Judah without the solicitation of a prostitute. But, no. Time and again, God chooses to tell his story through the monumentally poor choices of humanity. Take the entire book of Judges as an example.

Gideon: the self-described weakest member of the weakest tribe.

Samson: man, that guy was a train wreck.

Jephthah: in addition to having far too many "h"s in his name, he's the son of a prostitute.

Ehud: the left-handed son of the right.

Back to Jacob. Jacob obtains his father's blessing by pretending to be someone he is not.

"Who is it?" his father asks.

"Esau." Jacob responds.

Fast forward to Genesis 32:26–27. Jacob is wrestling for another blessing. This blessing is to come from his heavenly father rather than his earthly one. In verse 27, we see a variation of the same question from Genesis 27:18:

"What is your name?"

Surely, Jacob remembered the time his father asked him the same question back in Genesis 27...the time when he responded with a deceptive alternate identity. No doubt he remembered boldly lying to his father's face. "I'm Esau. I'm the man you want me to be. I'm not the meek, momma's boy who hates the outdoors. I'm the outdoorsman adventurer. I'm the burly killer of meats. I'm the Bear Grylls you want me to be."

I wonder what he thought as this angel posed the same question. "What is your name?" This time though, he answered truthfully: "Jacob." Deceiver. Trickster. Defrauder. This time, he was not blessed through his deception, but through his honesty — through his admission of who and what he was. Broken.

But, the Genesis 32 story of blessing through confession begins here in Genesis 27 with a blessing through deception. Jacob lies, deceives, and schemes; and yet, he received the inheritance and God's blessing. That gives me hope for the future.

AMP up your study of Genesis 27

Apply — Jacob spent years pretending to be someone he wasn't in order to receive a blessing he didn't think he could get as himself. Where in your life are you still performing, pretending, or presenting a version of yourself to God or others that isn't fully true? This week, practice one act of radical honesty — with God, with yourself, or with someone close to you.

Meditate — God used Jacob's story not despite his deception but straight through it. The line of Jesus runs through a con artist. What does that say about the kind of raw material God is willing to work with? How does that change the way you see your own failures and the failures of the people around you?

Pray — Pray the prayer Jacob couldn't pray yet — the honest one. Not "I am Esau" but "I am Jacob." Tell God exactly who you are, what you've done, and where you're broken. Then ask for the blessing anyway. Because that's exactly how it works.

Next week: Genesis Chapter 28 — Jacob's Ladder

Chapter Twenty-Eight

Week Twenty-Eight: Jacob's Ladder

Genesis Chapter 28

At the end of chapter 27, Rebekah hears that Esau plans to kill Jacob. So, she encourages Jacob to run away to his uncle Laban. In Genesis 28, Jacob has a dream while he is on the way to his uncle Laban's house. In this dream, he sees a stairway to Heaven with angels ascending and descending on it. He believes it to be the gateway to Heaven.

"He was afraid and said, 'How awesome is this place! This is none other than the house of God; this is the gate of heaven.'" (Genesis 28:17, NIV)

So, here's the scene: Jacob is probably terrified. He's running away from certain death. And, it's pretty much his fault his life is in danger. He lies down to rest, falls asleep, and has a dream of a ladder that could take him from earth to Heaven.

We've all felt like that at one point or another. We sit in anguish on this earth as we walk through some trial or pain. Maybe it was of our own making. Maybe not. But, we would give anything for a way out. And, that's the picture here: sin is seeking to destroy us. We're fleeing and scared. We'd love a path from death to life. We'd love some sort of escape hatch from this messy world...from the troubles of this world to Heaven. Wouldn't it be glorious if something like that just appeared out of nowhere and we could just climb it to escape this miserable earth?

Fast forward to the New Testament, to the life of Jesus and the first chapter of John.

Verse 51 is the relevant verse here. But first, I can't help but address one of my favorite answers in all of the Bible. It comes just a few verses prior.

"Philip found Nathanael and told him, 'We have found the one Moses wrote about in the Law, and about whom the prophets also wrote — Jesus of Nazareth, the son of Joseph.' 'Nazareth! Can anything good come from there?' Nathanael asked. 'Come and see,' said Philip." (John 1:45–46, NIV)

Philip doesn't answer with logical arguments or science. There's no nod to theory. There's no indulgence of rumors. There's no flattery. There are simply three little words that are probably the best answer anyone can give in the midst of a discussion or argument. "Come and see."

On to verse 51. Here, Jesus says something a bit odd.

"He then added, 'Very truly I tell you, you will see heaven open, and the angels of God ascending and descending on the Son of Man.'" (John 1:51, NIV)

It's a nod to Genesis 28:12. Same wording. Jesus is claiming to be Jacob's ladder...the very gateway to Heaven.

Jesus is saying that he is the solution to humanity's entire existential problem. Did your terrible life choices cause you to flee certain death like Jacob? Are you stressed? Are you at your wit's end? Do you want a pathway out of the mess? Do you desperately want a ladder out of the pit and up to Heaven? I think all humans feel this need for a way out at some point in their lives. Some more than others. Jacob sees the way out in Genesis 28. Jesus claims to be the way out in John 1. "Follow me," he says. I'm the ladder. I'm the way. I'm the bridge between Heaven and earth.

You may be asking the same thing that Nathanael asked...or, at least questions that echo Nathanael's:

"So, you're telling me that I desperately need an escape hatch from this life? Someone to bring life out of death and hope out of despair? And, you're telling me that there is such a way out? And, you're telling me it's some Jewish nomad from some podunk town in the middle of the east?"

My answer is the same as Philip's. "Come and see."

You cannot imagine the depth and the pain of the suffering in my life. Almost on cue, my son's oxygen alarm went off before I could finish this sentence. I wish I was making that up.

Six years ago, I was playing catch in the front yard with my boy. Tonight, he isn't able to swallow, and something is causing him to salivate constantly. It is causing a vicious cycle of essentially drowning himself, choking, coughing, then seizing. The suction machine has barely stopped running as I clear his saliva out of his trach every minute or so. He's had 10–20 seizures over the past hour. As he remains unable to move any of his limbs, I reposition his torso, head, both legs, and both arms after every cough and seizure. This chapter, like many of the others in this devotional, was written in fits and starts in the midst of the chaos — hence the title of this book. I counted how many times I stopped and started typing this paragraph alone. So far, 8. I can't count the number of nights where my wife or I — one or both of us — have endured this cycle for hours on end. If you're a parent, you know that I cannot adequately describe how hard this is. Pure torture.

So, why on earth do I answer, "Come and see?" Because, amidst our chaos, there is peace. There should be no peace. My wife and I should not be standing. Our family should not be standing. We exhausted the limits of our own strength years ago. I say, "Come and see" because Christianity is packed with stories like ours. In the face of the worst kinds of suffering imaginable, the hopeless find hope. The broken find joy. The restless find peace. The blind see. The deaf hear. The lame walk. The dead are raised. Addictions are broken. Relationships are restored. That's the foreshadowing we find in Genesis 28. When you've reached the end of your proverbial rope, you'll find that there is a way, there is a truth, and there is a life.

"There have always been, as there are today, people who try to solve the problem of suffering by denying the sovereignty of God — that is the all-ruling providence of God over Satan and over nature and over human hearts and deeds. But it is

remarkable how many of those who stand by the doctrine of God's sovereignty over suffering have been those who suffered most and who found in the doctrine the most comfort and help." — John Piper

AMP up your study of Genesis 28

Apply — Philip's answer to Nathanael's skepticism was simply "Come and see." Think of one person in your life who is skeptical about faith — not hostile, just unconvinced. This week, instead of arguing or explaining, invite them to witness something. Bring them along somewhere. Show them, don't tell them.

Meditate — Jacob was running for his life, exhausted and terrified, when he saw the ladder. God didn't show up when Jacob had it together — he showed up in the middle of the flight. When was the last time you encountered God most clearly not in a moment of peace, but in the middle of your own desperate running?

Pray — If you are in a season of chaos right now — real, unrelenting, not-what-you-planned chaos — pray the words of Psalm 46:1 this week: *"God is our refuge and strength, an ever-present help in trouble."* Pray it out loud. More than once. Let it be the ladder when the ground feels like it's gone.

Next week: Genesis Chapter 29 — The Deceiver Is Deceived

Chapter Twenty-Nine

Week Twenty-Nine: The Deceiver Is Deceived

Genesis Chapter 29

I'll start with a brief synopsis of Genesis 29, Josh's Revised Abbreviated Version. Jacob falls for Rachel and agrees to work 7 years for his uncle, Laban, in exchange for marrying her. After 7 years, Jacob finally marries. But, in a bizarre twist — the Bible is full of bizarre twists — he accidentally marries her lazy-eyed sister, Leah. Then, he works 7 more years in exchange for Rachel. Side note: as is often the case in the Bible, none of the main characters in this story take on the role of "hero." All of the characters have flaws.

Do you know what I don't remember as a kid? I don't remember ever sitting in Bible class or listening to a sermon or reading my Bible and thinking, "Man, this stuff is incredibly messed up."

Reading Genesis as an adult though, there are very few chapters where I haven't had that thought. "Man, this stuff is pretty messed up."

Genesis 29 is, well, another one of those chapters.

Jacob thought he was making a deal to marry Rachel, but when the light of day came, he realized he was with Leah. Was he drunk? If so, exactly how drunk was he? I mean, there's "buzzed and over-celebrating a Dallas Cowboys touchdown" and then there's "I got married and slept with the wrong woman" drunk. Maybe she was veiled as I've heard was the custom those days. Or maybe he was, in fact, just really drunk. Maybe both. Who knows? Anyway, talk about morning-after confusion and regret.

I have a few thoughts here. First of all, I'm betting that Jacob would have most likely immediately realized the parallel between deceiving his father and being deceived by Laban. If you'll recall in chapter 27, his father, Isaac, couldn't see. Jacob convinced Isaac that he was with one person (Esau) when he was in fact with another person (Jacob). Laban pulled a similar trick. This time, Jacob finds himself in the dark. Instead of being old with weak eyes, he was unable to see for other reasons. Jacob was told he was with one person (Rachel) when he was, in fact, with another (Leah). Although I doubt Leah would refer to the act as receiving Jacob's blessing, this is in essence the natural consequence of procreation...possible co-creation of your firstborn...who, traditionally, would receive your blessing. In other words, thanks to Laban's deception, Jacob's blessing could ultimately go to the wrong person...to Leah's child rather than Rachel's. I bet Jacob saw the irony.

In parenting and in life, the times I've been most frustrated with something or someone, God was trying to teach me something about my own flaws. Every time. Here's a good habit: the times in life when you're most frustrated with someone — as Jacob was with Laban — I think it's good to pause and reflect. Is there something God is trying to show you or teach you? Nothing stinks more than that moment you realize you're wrong in an argument or in life. But, what if God is trying to show you something about your own life in these moments of frustration...moments of high emotion...moments where someone has just pulled a fast one on you and you accidentally slept with the wrong woman?

I'll give you an example from my life.

As all kids do, my kids love playing with empty boxes. Some years, the boxes get more play time than the Christmas gift they contained. Why didn't we just wrap up empty boxes instead of spending money on gifts? I digress. Many years ago, one of my daughters — who was around 2 years old at the time — was playing with a box that, when she stood in it, came up to just above her knees. For some reason she decided to put the box on her head and run around in circles. All of a sudden, she stopped and turned to face a wall that was 10 feet in front of her. Then, blinded by the box on her head, she proceeded to run full speed into the wall. SMACK. I wasn't fast enough to stop her.

There she lay, moaning and sprawled out on the floor, with the box still somehow covering her head and shoulders. I hear a muffled and tearful "Daddy, I've got an owie." from inside the box. Part of me was concerned about whether or not she was injured — she wasn't; just a bruise. The other part of me was thinking, "Well, of course you've got an owie. You just stuck a box over your head and ran full speed into a wall. How was this possibly going to end well?!"

Later on, I asked myself the question, "What can I learn about myself from this situation?"

At the time I was incredibly stressed and exhausted. All the time. Most of my prayers went something like this: "God, please take away my stress. I'm so unbearably tired. Please grant me some rest." In other words, my prayers were the grown-up version of "Daddy, I've got an owie."

Then, I surveyed my life. Between my day job, side businesses, boards, church, family, home renovation projects, etc., I was absurdly over-committed. I'd said "Sure, I can help you with that," to pretty much anyone who asked. Tip: saying "Sure, I can help you with that," isn't a blessing to anyone if you don't have the time to do it well. In fact, you're actually — while well-meaningly — becoming a roadblock to whomever you agreed to help.

The lesson: I was doing exactly what my daughter had done. I'd put a box on my head, ran into a wall, then whined about having an owie. I wasn't hurting because God wasn't granting me peace or rest or sleep or stress relief. I was hurting because I foolishly ran myself full speed into a wall. I kind of feel like God was just shaking his head at my prayers. "Well, of course you're stressed and tired. You committed to 37 hours a day worth of work. How was this possibly going to end well? Try taking the box off of your head and not running around like a crazy person."

So, that is one of my takeaways from Genesis 29. If I'm honest about the times in my life where I've been most frustrated with someone or something, there's been an issue in my own life that I needed to refine. Thanks for the painful reminder, Genesis 29.

Here's my second takeaway from this chapter.

As we get to the end of chapter 29, Leah seems to put all her hopes on Jacob loving her. The text basically says, "If I can just have a child for him, he'll finally love me. If I can just have a child, everything in my world will be right. I'll finally have peace." Three times in verses 32 through 34. Each time, she realizes that accomplishing her goal leaves her unfulfilled.

We all do the same thing. For some, it's children. For others, it's career. For others, it's a relationship. For others, it's money. "If I can just have _______, everything in my world will be right and I'll have peace."

Something in Leah changes though. In verse 35, her tone changes. *"This time I will praise the Lord."* (NIV) It's as if she has made a mental shift to acknowledge where ultimate peace comes from. When she finally lays down her empty desires and opts to praise God anyway, she gives birth to Judah...the tribe of Jesus.

Perhaps that's a good place to end this week and a good lesson to take away from Genesis 29. Is there something outside of Jesus in which we're pinning our hopes for a bright future? Fame? Money? Power? Spouse? Kids? All those things will be found wanting. I'll leave you with two quotes from highly successful people who discovered this the hard way:

"If you pin your self-love and happiness to something external, you'll either keep moving the finish line and never be happy or you'll experience the most profound anticlimax in your life and get depressed when you realize that achieving your external goal does not fill the inner void." — Ash Ali

And from an interview with Tom Brady:

"There's times where I'm not the person that I want to be. Why do I have three Super Bowl rings, and still think there's something greater out there for me? I mean, maybe a lot of people would say, 'Hey man, this is what is.' I reached my

goal, my dream, my life. Me, I think: God, it's gotta be more than this. I mean this can't be what it's all cracked up to be. I mean I've done it. I'm 27. And what else is there for me?"

Interviewer: *"What's the answer?"*

Brady: *"I wish I knew. I wish I knew..."*

AMP up your study of Genesis 29

Apply — Take the box off your head. This week, look honestly at your calendar and your commitments. Where have you over-promised, over-committed, or said yes when God was asking you to say no? Identify one thing you can step back from — and actually do it.

Meditate — Fill in the blank honestly: "If I can just have _________, everything in my world will be right and I'll finally have peace." Now ask yourself: what has that thing actually delivered when you've gotten it before? What does your answer reveal about where you're really looking for peace?

Pray — Pray Leah's prayer: *"This time I will praise the Lord."* Say it even if you don't feel it yet. Pray it over the unfulfilled thing in your life — the thing you've been waiting on to finally make everything okay. Ask God to be enough before the thing arrives, not after.

Next week: Genesis Chapter 30 — A Battle of the Wombs

Chapter Thirty

Week Thirty: A Battle of the Wombs

Genesis Chapter 30

Genesis 30 begins with a baby battle between two wives. Rachel and Leah are fighting it out to see who can give Jacob the most sons...whether by their own doing or by having him sleep with their servants.

At no point does Jacob step in and say, "Whoa whoa whoa, ladies. Let's all calm down a minute." In fact, we don't see any objection from him at all.

In verses 15 and 16, we have two of my favorite lines in all of scripture.

"But she said to her, 'Is it a small matter that you have taken away my husband? Would you take away my son's mandrakes also?' Rachel said, 'Then he may lie with you tonight in exchange for your son's mandrakes.' When Jacob came from the field in the evening, Leah went out to meet him and said, 'You must come in to me, for I have hired you with my son's mandrakes.' So he lay with her that night." (Genesis 30:15–16, ESV)

This is one of those stories that gives credence to my belief that the Bible is true. These are details no sane person would put in a story that had been fabricated. What we see here is, again, no objection whatsoever from Jacob. You would expect some sort of dialogue here. "Wait...Rachel would rather have mandrakes than share a bed with me? Wait. What?! Ah, c'mon!" Nothing. Just prolific acquiescence.

Unsurprisingly, the power struggle between Rachel and Leah extended to their offspring. From this point on, we'll see jealousy, infighting, and strife between these brothers. Eventually, we'll even see civil war between their descendants. But, there's an interesting twist. Verse 22:

"Then God remembered Rachel, and God listened to her and opened her womb. She conceived and bore a son and said, 'God has taken away my reproach.' And she called his name Joseph, saying, 'May the Lord add to me another son!'" (Genesis 30:22–24, ESV)

In the midst of a battle between women, God listens to Rachel. I'm going to jump ahead a bit because I think it's important to reflect on how important this chapter is in the grand scheme of things. It's important because the son God gives Rachel in verse 23 would be the savior of the entire family line...including Leah's son Judah. Of course, this is a rather important turn of events for Christianity. Without Judah, we've got a problem, theologically speaking. No Judah, no Jesus.

Let's summarize the story that begins in this chapter. God puts life in Rachel's barren womb. This life, Joseph, is despised by his brothers to the point that they strip him of his dignity, sell him out for twenty pieces of silver, and abandon him to die. Despite this, Joseph ends up miraculously rising to power in the land of Egypt. As a reminder, Egypt in the Bible is often a parallel for a sinful, oppressive place...a symbol for the fallen world. Joseph rises to power there and controls the food supply, ultimately giving him the power to give life or withhold it from his family...and pretty much everyone else. Joseph's brothers feel that starvation is coming due to famine, so they head to Egypt to beg for mercy. They don't recognize their brother...mainly because they didn't expect him to come to power...and certainly not after they abandoned him. Joseph eventually saves them all in a remarkable act of grace.

Of course, this sets the stage for Jesus's role in God's ultimate salvation plan. Jesus is woven into the fabric of the Joseph story; or, actually, it's the other way around.

Genesis 30 yet again reminded me that the story of Jesus is the greatest story ever told. And, the Jesus story wasn't confined to the Gospels. The story began in Genesis 1:1. The plot thickens in Genesis 30. The story flows through the past, present, and future. And here's the best news: today, you and I are both observers of and participants in that same salvation story.

AMP up your study of Genesis 30

Apply — Rachel waited. She competed, she strived, she watched her sister win round after round — and then quietly, God remembered her. This week, write down one thing you have been waiting on God to remember. Date it. Pray over it specifically. Then put it somewhere you'll find it again in a year.

Meditate — "God remembered Rachel." In the middle of a competition she was losing, a marriage that was complicated, and a life that wasn't going the way she'd hoped — God remembered her. Is there an area of your life where you've started to wonder if God has forgotten you? What would it mean to believe that he remembers?

Pray — Pray for the Joseph in your life — the person or thing God has placed in your story whose full significance you may not yet understand. Ask God to protect it, grow it, and use it in ways you can't currently see. Then pray for the grace to trust the story even when you're stuck in chapter 30.

Next week: Genesis Chapter 31 — Jacob Flees Laban

Chapter Thirty-One

Week Thirty-One: Stolen Gods

Genesis Chapter 31

Genesis 31 gives us two takeaways worth sitting with this week.

The first involves Rachel's theft of her father's household idols. Why did Rachel steal her father Laban's gods? The Bible doesn't say directly, but historical evidence from the ancient Near East offers a compelling explanation: she may have wanted his inheritance. Archaeological records, including cuneiform tablets from the ancient Mesopotamian site of Nuzi — documented in James B. Pritchard's *Ancient Near Eastern Texts Relating to the Old Testament* — indicate that possession of household gods could entitle a son-in-law to claim a deceased father-in-law's estate under certain conditions. This suggests Rachel might have taken the household idols to secure inheritance rights for Jacob, given Laban's long and deceptive treatment of them.

What I find funny is that Laban doesn't seem to see the irony in his stolen gods. If your god can be stolen from you, it's probably time to find a better god.

The second takeaway is the contrast between Laban and Jacob. The picture Genesis paints of Laban is that he is a real piece of work. He basically does his best to wring every last drop of work and money out of Jacob that he can.

Each move to extort more work out of Jacob somehow ends up transferring more wealth from Laban to Jacob. Laban grows poorer — losing kids, animals, food, etc. Jacob grows wealthier — gaining kids, animals, food, etc. It seems that Laban spends his days pinching pennies, cheating his employees, and squandering his wealth. Meanwhile, we see a picture of Jacob sacrificing and sharing his wealth with all of his relatives in verse 54.

"He offered a sacrifice there in the hill country and invited his relatives to a meal. After they had eaten, they spent the night there." (Genesis 31:54, NIV)

Put simply: Laban loved money and used people. Jacob loved people and used money.

Genesis 31:54 reminds me of Luke 16:9: *"I tell you, use worldly wealth to gain friends for yourselves, so that when it is gone, you will be welcomed into eternal dwellings."* (NIV)

That's a good reminder for me today. It's both a personal and a business challenge. I want to be known as a person who loves people and uses money — not the other way around.

AMP up your study of Genesis 31

Apply — Laban loved money and used people. Jacob loved people and used money. Be honest: which one more accurately describes your default posture — at work, at home, in your community? This week, find one specific way to use your money or resources to invest in a person rather than a transaction.

Meditate — Rachel stole her father's gods and sat on them. She was holding onto a false source of security even as she fled toward something better. What are the household idols you're still carrying — the things you're holding onto for security that God has already rendered powerless in your life?

Pray — Ask God to reveal any area where you've been treating money as a master rather than a tool. Pray for the generosity of Jacob — the kind that invites people to the table, shares what you have, and trusts God to replenish it. Then find someone to feed this week, literally or figuratively.

Next week: Genesis Chapter 32 — Jacob Wrestles with God

Chapter Thirty-Two

Week Thirty-Two: Who Are You?

Genesis Chapter 32

On Jacob's journey back to his homeland, he passes through his brother's land. Though he had been away for over 20 years, he is still worried about Esau's desire to kill him; so, he approaches with extreme caution. He stays on one side of a stream and first sends a procession of gifts. Eventually, he sends everything and everyone across the stream ahead of him, procrastinating his meeting with his brother, Esau. Jacob is left completely alone. Then, alone with his thoughts and fears, he wrestles with God all night.

It's important to jump back to Genesis 27. In Genesis 27, Jacob is asked the same question by his earthly father that he is asked by his heavenly father here in Genesis 32.

"Who are you, my son?" Isaac asks in verse 18. Jacob's response: *"I am Esau your firstborn."* (verse 19). Jacob doubles down on the lie in verse 24.

"Are you really my son Esau?" he asked. *"I am,"* he replied. (Genesis 27:24, NIV)

I bet Jacob is thinking about this moment when he is again asked who he is in Genesis 32:27.

"The man asked him, 'What is your name?' 'Jacob,' he answered." (Genesis 32:27, NIV)

This time, he answers honestly. There is no more hiding. He is owning up to who he is — I think literally and symbolically. Jacob means supplanter, heel grabber, deceiver, over-reacher. He is owning up to being all of those things.

It seems that Jacob has been wrestling with God and himself...with who he was as a person...his identity. In that moment of admission comes blessing. One moment, he admits who he is. The next moment — the next verse — God tells him who he will be.

"Then the man said, 'Your name will no longer be Jacob, but Israel, because you have struggled with God and with humans and have overcome.'" (Genesis 32:28, NIV)

In the Bible, blessing often follows confession or humility.

Here's the first takeaway this week: even if you put on a brave face for the rest of the world, it's important to be honest with God about who you are...especially in those moments where you're wrestling with something or someone. God has a habit of stepping into those moments of humble vulnerability and using them as pivot points for his glory. Whether it's Jacob in the darkness, Peter on the beach, Saul on the road to Damascus, a Samaritan at a well, Jonah in a fish, Zacchaeus in a tree, or Job in agony. Who are you? I'm Josh. I'm a prideful sinner too often focused on my own glory. I'm in need of mercy, grace, forgiveness, and guidance.

The second takeaway comes from verses 25 and 31:

"When the man saw that he could not overpower him, he touched the socket of Jacob's hip so that his hip was wrenched as he wrestled with the man."

"The sun rose above him as he passed Peniel, and he was limping because of his hip." (Genesis 32:25, 31 NIV)

A friend told me a story of a time he was riding mountain bikes in the canyon with a friend. At one point during the ride, he was really struggling to pedal. They stopped for a minute on the side of the trail. He was sweating like crazy and struggling for breath. Oddly, his friend didn't appear tired or struggling for breath at all. That's when he looked down at his bike tire and noticed something.

His brake was stuck against the wheel. He had been pedaling with his brake on. No wonder he was exhausted.

That's a good analogy for my life. For the past 6 years, I feel as though the brake has been stuck against the wheel of my life. Sleep evades us. I can count on one hand the number of times we left the house together as a family from 2022 until 2024. Every single task of our lives is 10x more challenging mentally, emotionally, physically, and spiritually than it was prior to 2021. We can't quite get the brake off of the wheel. We walk with a limp.

The longer I limp through this life, the more I realize that everyone has a limp. Everyone is dealing with some sort of pain, tragedy, setback, or battle. Everyone. It's just that some people are better at disguising it than others.

Jacob walked with a literal limp. Paul walked with a spiritual thorn in his flesh. I walk with emotional trauma few understand. I bet you walk with some challenge, too. In fact, I bet if your harshest critics knew about the particular challenge you're walking with, they'd applaud you instead of criticize you.

My encouragement today: God shows up and shows off in our weakness — whether he chooses to take away our weakness or chooses to strengthen us and others by it. He used Israel with a limp. Paul with a thorn. Moses with a speech impediment. Peter with impulse control issues. Rahab with poor occupational life choices. Joseph with a prison sentence. A Samaritan woman with all kinds of issues. David with a lust issue. Gideon with weakness of lineage. Sarah and Rebekah and Rachel and Hannah and Mary with barren wombs. And, in one of my favorite turns of events, God uses a ragamuffin band of 12 politically and socioeconomically diverse people — each with all kinds of issues — to change the world.

AMP up your study of Genesis 32

Apply — Jacob's blessing came the moment he stopped pretending and told the truth about who he was. This week, have one honest conversation — with God, with yourself, or with someone you trust — where you stop saying "I am Esau" and start saying "I am Jacob." Name your actual struggle out loud. See what happens next.

Meditate — Everyone has a limp. What's yours? And more importantly — how has God used it, or how might he use it, in ways that wouldn't be possible if you were walking without one? Think about someone whose limp you know about. How does knowing it change the way you see them?

Pray — Pray the honest prayer: not the polished Sunday morning version, but the 3 a.m., wrestling-all-night version. Ask God to meet you in the dark. Ask him to rename you — to tell you who you will be, not just who you've been. Then listen.

Next week: Genesis Chapter 33 — Jacob and Esau Reunite

Chapter Thirty-Three

Week Thirty-Three: Jacob and Esau Reunite

Genesis Chapter 33

Last week we talked about Genesis 32, where Jacob is preparing to meet Esau — scared to the point of death and wrestling with God all night. In Genesis 33, the dreaded meeting with Esau finally occurs. In an effort to protect his family, Jacob divides up the group — placing them in order of importance to him...which is totally a jerk move.

"Jacob looked up and there was Esau, coming with his four hundred men; so he divided the children among Leah, Rachel and the two female servants. He put the female servants and their children in front, Leah and her children next, and Rachel and Joseph in the rear. He himself went on ahead and bowed down to the ground seven times as he approached his brother." (Genesis 33:1–3, NIV)

Can you imagine being one of Leah's kids and being like, "Hey, what the heck, Dad?" Anyhow, at least he had the guts to go first.

To me, this is yet another moment of the Old Testament being a physical representation of a spiritual reality. You can sense the fear and terror of Jacob. He is legitimately concerned for his life. He has stolen from, deceived, and betrayed his twin brother...and his father. Not only is he afraid for his life, but the weight of guilt is hitting him. Genesis 33 does a great job of putting the reader in Jacob's shoes and making us feel his fear, terror, dread, and guilt. Then, in an instant, when he was most expecting death, he receives life. A pardon of sorts. Forgiveness. Relief.

The language used in verse 4 is remarkably similar to Luke 15:20 — the story of the Prodigal Son. I discussed this connection a bit back in chapter 25, but since this is my book and I do what I want, I'm going to be redundant and talk about it again here. You're welcome.

There are a number of parallels to the Luke 15 story in the Jacob and Esau narrative. Verse 10 carries the same feeling as the prodigal son story — that sense of relief one feels when they fear the worst and are instead rewarded with the best. *"No, please!"* said Jacob. *"If I have found favor in your eyes, accept this gift from me. For to see your face is like seeing the face of God, now that you have received me favorably."* (Genesis 33:10, NIV)

For me, this chapter is a reminder. A reminder that every single moment in this life that produces any semblance of those feelings — fear, dread, terror — Christianity teaches that those moments are met with the exact opposite. Here's the best part: even when those feelings stem from my own monumental idiocy, Jesus meets me with grace, forgiveness, and peace. Good news for Jacob. Good news for the prodigal son. Good news for you and me.

It's refreshing. It's relieving. It's life giving.

AMP up your study of Genesis 33

Apply — Is there a person in your life you've been avoiding — someone you wronged, drifted from, or are afraid to face? This week, take one step toward them. It doesn't have to be the full reconciliation. Just stop running in the other direction. Send the message. Make the call. Make the first move.

Meditate — Jacob expected death and received grace. The prodigal son expected a servant's quarters and received a party. When has God surprised you with grace when you were braced for punishment? How does remembering that moment change the way you approach God right now?

Pray — Pray for the Esau in your life — the person you've wronged and perhaps haven't faced yet. Ask God to prepare the way for reconciliation, to soften the ground, and to give you the courage to stop hiding behind your processions of gifts and actually show up.

Next week: Genesis Chapter 34 — Brothers' Revenge

Chapter Thirty-Four

Week Thirty-Four: Brothers' Revenge

Genesis Chapter 34

Well, here's a fun chapter. This is another one of those stories that you will find in exactly zero illustrated children's Bibles. Allow me to give you a brief synopsis:

A couple of Jacob's sons get mad at a dude for defiling their sister. So, they basically trick an entire city into getting circumcised — which is some trick, by the way — and then, after all the men of the city actually do this and begin the post-circumcision healing process, the brothers use this moment of maximum pain and weakness to strut into the city and murder each and every one of them. Jacob's like, "Boys! What in the world?! You've enraged basically everyone surrounding us. What if they decide to band together and come after us? They'll kill us all. What on earth were you thinking? How could you do this to our family?" I absolutely love the boys' response to their father: "Well, they shouldn't have defiled our sister."

First of all, I find it a little suspect that Jacob was the kind of father who let his young daughter freely roam around amidst the depravity of the Shechemites. I suppose there's a chance that she snuck out or something. The Bible doesn't really say. Regardless, there is little to no chance that the Israelites were not aware of the depravity of the Shechemite people. Zero chance Dinah roams around the area without something bad happening. Where was Jacob?

A modern-day parenting parallel might be giving your Dinah-aged daughter unrestricted access to a phone. Zero chance she scrolls social media without something bad happening. Sorry, I thought it would be fun to offend some parents mid-chapter. You're welcome.

Back to the story. While the story highlights the actions of the brothers, my focus stays on the father, Jacob. I feel like he fails at every turn here. Whether or not he let his daughter roam free amongst depravity or she snuck out, verse 5 tells us that he did nothing about it when he found out what happened. How do you act so detached? It's sort of like he's too cowardly to do anything, so he waits until his hot-headed sons get home to let them enact judgment. Then, when the father of Dinah's abuser comes to talk things over, Jacob basically steps out and hands the discussion over to his hot-headed sons. It takes his boys killing every single male in the city for Jacob to finally step up and say something.

"Then Jacob said to Simeon and Levi, 'You have brought trouble on me by making me obnoxious to the Canaanites and Perizzites, the people living in this land. We are few in number, and if they join forces against me and attack me, I and my household will be destroyed.'" (Genesis 34:30, NIV)

I mean, he's not wrong; but where was this outrage when his daughter was raped?

So, what do I feel like God is trying to get across to me this week?

Dads aren't called to be passive observers of family dynamics. They are called to lead, protect, advocate for, and defend. Whether it's protecting my daughter from social media or my sons from murdering an entire city, sometimes you have to step up as a parent, toss aside your own fears, and lead your family forward through hard things.

AMP up your study of Genesis 34

Apply — Where have you been a passive observer in your family when the situation called for leadership? It doesn't have to be dramatic — sometimes it's as simple as initiating a hard conversation you've been avoiding, setting a boundary you've been too tired to enforce, or showing up when it's inconvenient. Identify one place this week where your family needs you to lead rather than wait.

Meditate — Jacob's inaction didn't prevent chaos — it just delayed it and made it worse. Where in your life has passivity created bigger problems than the discomfort of acting sooner would have? What does it cost the people around you when you choose to stay silent or stay out of it?

Pray — Ask God for the courage to be a protector — not a controller, but a genuine guardian of the people in your care. Pray for the wisdom to know when to step in and when to step back, and for the discernment to tell the difference before the city gets burned down.

Next week: Genesis Chapter 35 — Return to Bethel

Chapter Thirty-Five

Week Thirty-Five: Old and Full of Years

Genesis Chapter 35

Genesis 35 is a chapter full of burial. First, Jacob buries all the foreign gods of his crew under an oak tree. Then, Rebekah's nurse dies and is buried under a different oak tree. Then, Rachel dies as she gives birth to the last of the patriarchs of the 12 tribes of Israel — she is buried on the way to Bethlehem. Lastly, Isaac dies and is buried in Hebron.

Aside from all the burials, here are a couple other highlights: as Rachel is dying in childbirth, she names her son Ben-Oni, which means "son of my trouble." Jacob names him Benjamin instead, which means "son of my right hand." And, Jacob's son Reuben sleeps with one of his father's concubines, Bilhah. That's pretty messed up, even for the Bible. It is worth noting that this was a practice in pagan culture — sleeping with the father's concubine was a show of power and a symbolic transition of family authority to the son who would be taking over.

In the midst of all the death and dysfunction in this chapter, five words stood out more than the others this week. They are the words *"old and full of years"* from verse 29.

"Then he breathed his last and died and was gathered to his people, old and full of years. And his sons Esau and Jacob buried him." (Genesis 35:29, NIV)

Abraham is described the same way in Genesis 25:8. Old and full of years.

We see these words again in Job 42:17: *"And so Job died, an old man and full of years."* (NIV)

King David is described the same way twice: during his life in 1 Chronicles 23:1 and at his death in 1 Chronicles 29:28. Old and full of years.

The phrase begs the question: how do you make your life full of years as opposed to empty of years?

I'm one of those nerds who is big on long-term goal setting. I like 5-year plans. I like 10-year plans. I like planning time to plan my plans. This chapter was great for me to ponder because exactly zero of these guys whose lives were described as "old and full of years"...zero of their lives went according to their plans. Abraham. Isaac. Job. David. They lived some extreme highs and lows. To quote the great philosopher Mike Tyson, "Everyone has a plan until they get punched in the mouth." Each of those guys got punched in the mouth. Repeatedly. It's not that long-term planning is bad. It's just that it can't be the key to a life that is "full of years."

Personally, I think a life full of years hinges upon shorter-term habits rather than longer-term plans. Old Testament Jews were notoriously ritualistic. Reading Torah is a habit. Praying is a habit. Seeking God is a habit. Shared meals are a habit. Kindness to sojourners is a habit. Sacrifice is a habit. Offerings are a habit. Solid daily habits were engrained into the lives of Abraham, Isaac, Job, and David in times of feast and famine.

Actually, it's interesting how often the Bible as a whole focuses on the present as opposed to long-term future planning. The Israelites were to keep lamps burning daily (Exodus 27:21), sacrifice daily (Exodus 29:38), and burn incense daily (Exodus 30:7). God's mercies are made new every morning (Lamentations 3:22–23). We are to take up our crosses daily (Luke 9:23). We are to rejoice and be glad today (Psalm 118:24). We are to ask God to give us this day our daily bread (Matthew 6:11). The Israelites were to talk about the commands of God daily (Deuteronomy 6:7). Elijah was sustained by food from ravens day by day (1

Kings 17:6). Manna in the wilderness lasted for one day before spoiling (Exodus 16).

All that said, my takeaway from Genesis 35 this week was a simple but powerful reminder: make sure I'm focusing more on creating good daily habits than on creating a perfect 10-year plan.

Since his book *Atomic Habits* is top of mind for me this week, I'll leave you with four of my favorite James Clear quotes:

"The implicit assumption behind any goal is this: 'Once I reach my goal, then I'll be happy.' The problem with a goals-first mentality is that you're continually putting happiness off until the next milestone."

"Your outcomes are a lagging measure of your habits. Your net worth is a lagging measure of your financial habits. Your weight is a lagging measure of your eating habits. Your knowledge is a lagging measure of your learning habits. Your clutter is a lagging measure of your cleaning habits. You get what you repeat."

"Every action you take is a vote for the type of person you wish to become. No single instance will transform your beliefs, but as the votes build up, so does the evidence of your new identity."

"You do not rise to the level of your goals. You fall to the level of your systems."

AMP up your study of Genesis 35

Apply — Pick one daily habit this week — just one — that you want to be true of your life when someone describes you as "old and full of years." Not a goal, not a resolution, not a 10-year plan. A single daily practice. Start it today. Do it again tomorrow.

Meditate — "Old and full of years." What's the difference between a long life and a full one? Think of someone you know who is older and whose life seems genuinely full — not necessarily prosperous or easy, but full. What habits do you observe in them? What do they prioritize that others don't?

Pray — Ask God to show you the daily habits he wants to build into your life — the rhythms of prayer, Scripture, generosity, rest, and relationship that will make your years full rather than merely long. Then ask for the discipline to actually do them on the ordinary days, not just the inspired ones.

Next week: Genesis Chapter 36 — The Line of Esau

Chapter Thirty-Six

Week Thirty-Six: The Fate of the Edomites

Genesis Chapter 36

Genesis 36 gives an overview of Esau's descendants — the Edomites. Esau is presented in many ways as the opposite of his brother, Jacob. Esau is described as sort of this hairy, calloused, manly man type of guy. Hunter. Gatherer. Outdoorsman. Jacob was more of a homebody and momma's boy. I get the sense that Jacob harbored a bit of jealousy toward the type of manly man Esau was...and particularly the attention Esau received from their father. Of course, Jacob is presented as the "winner" — albeit by deception — in the sibling rivalry. He got the blessing. He got the birthright.

Given Jacob's "victories" over his brother, Genesis 36 is a little, well, surprising. Genesis 36 covers about a 400-year time period. It seems to me that, for basically all of that time, it looked like Esau received the greater blessing than Jacob. He married the women he wanted to. He had a lot of kids. He became a great nation with lots of wealth and chiefs and kings. Meanwhile, Jacob also became a great nation, but walked with bitter heartache. The blessing he stole in Genesis 27:27–29 sounds great; but, if I were Jacob, life isn't going down the way I thought it would. I had the firstborn inheritance. I had the blessing. But,

I'm still living in fear of my brother, and — spoiler alert for chapter 37 — I'm mourning the death of a son.

Unfortunately, I know something myself about mourning a son. I can assure you that Jacob's grief put a cloud over his entire Genesis 27 blessing. Those blessed things like fatness of the earth, grain, wine, or nations bowing down to you...those things don't satisfy the same way when your son is gone. This is speculation; but I can imagine that Jacob wrestled with God more than a little over the frustration of getting everything he thought he wanted yet still feeling empty and afraid. Also, in the midst of this wrestling, he was probably hearing reports of the growing kingdom of Esau. No doubt that added to his inner frustration and turmoil.

Of course, we know the rest of the story. Things didn't go so well for the Edomites. Actually, things went about as terribly as things can go for a nation. Check out the book of Obadiah for details. The entire book is basically a diatribe and judgment against them. The great kingdom of Esau was, indeed, wiped from the face of the earth as prophesied...but not before the line of Jacob and Esau square off again in the New Testament. Herod the Great — the baby-killing Herod from the New Testament — was an Edomite. Spoiler alert. Israel wins. Jesus wins. We all win.

Israel became a great nation despite attempts in just about every generation to wipe them from the face of the earth. In modern times, we see remarkable life in the land and the people of Israel. A couple notable examples: anthropologically speaking, we have perhaps the only example in history of a dead language — Hebrew — coming back to usage and life. In the Jews, we have a historical anomaly of a people group that had been scattered across the globe only to reunify into an official nation. Not only that, with the establishment of the nation of Israel in 1948 we saw a literal transformation of desert land into fertility. From death to life. Language. Land. People. All transitioned from death to life. Meanwhile, the Edomites vanished. From life to death. It's almost as if our creator is trying to paint us a picture here.

That's my takeaway from Genesis 36 this week. It's the ultimate choice that all of humanity faces: are we moving from life to death; or, are we moving from death to life? Are we moving from silence to sound or sound to silence? Are we moving from desert to fertility or fertility to desert? I'm reminded to do my best each and every day to live up to the challenge I'm given in Ephesians 4:1: to live a life worthy of the calling I've received. By injecting life into my language. By injecting life into my home. By injecting life into the people around me.

AMP up your study of Genesis 36

Apply — Ephesians 4:1 challenges us to live a life worthy of our calling. This week, pick one relationship, one conversation, or one environment where you have been bringing death — criticism, cynicism, silence, absence — and choose to bring life instead. One deliberate act of life-giving in a place that's been dry.

Meditate — Jacob had the blessing and the birthright and still felt empty and afraid. Esau had what looked like the greater life for 400 years — and then it vanished. What does that say about what we're actually chasing when we chase worldly markers of success? What would it look like to measure your life by life-giving rather than life-accumulating?

Pray — Pray Ephesians 4:1 over your own life this week: *"I urge you to live a life worthy of the calling you have received."* Ask God to show you specifically where your daily habits are moving toward life and where they're quietly moving toward death. Ask for the courage to make the turn.

Next week: Genesis Chapter 37 — A Great Foreshadowing

Chapter Thirty-Seven

Week Thirty-Seven: A Great Foreshadowing

Genesis Chapter 37

Genesis 37 contains one of the most famous stories in the Bible.

I'll begin this week with a semi-irrelevant side note: in the early days of the internet, I heard about this new website called eBay where you could list items for sale. The first item I ever listed on eBay was my little brother — complete with a photo, list of pros and cons, and list of household chores he could complete. I couldn't find a buyer, so we kept him around.

But, I digress.

Everyone has brother-sister issues; but the sibling rivalries throughout the Bible are next-level...this one in Genesis 37 included. Here we have a story of jealousy so strong that it leads to a debate as to whether murder or human trafficking is the better option.

Of all people, you would think that Jacob would understand the pain of a father playing favorites and the havoc it creates. Nope.

"Now Israel loved Joseph more than any of his other sons, because he had been born to him in his old age; and he made an ornate robe for him. When his brothers

saw that their father loved him more than any of them, they hated him and could not speak a kind word to him." (Genesis 37:3–4, NIV)

I imagine that tossing Joseph in the cistern was the culmination of years of bullying and torment. When I was in 6th grade, I was bullied by a random 8th grader who was twice my size. That isn't saying much, because I was a tiny little middle schooler. Fortunately, I was never shoved into a locker; but I would have fit quite nicely. I had all the confidence that could fit into my frame, which was very little. Anyhow, I didn't have any prophetic dreams about my particular bully; but I know how it would have gone if I'd walked up to him and said, "I had this recurring dream where you bow down to me. My dream is telling me that I eventually become your ruler, loser." There is no scenario where that interaction wouldn't have ended in a wedgie. Probably an atomic one.

That said, it's a little surprising to me that Joseph had the confidence to share his dream with his brothers. But, he did. I do wonder how quickly it was during his disrobed time in the cistern that Joseph began to doubt the prophetic dreams he was so confident in. I wonder if, as his brothers walked away and he glanced around helplessly at the dark walls around him, he thought, "Well...I guess I interpreted those dreams wrong." Maybe he didn't doubt. I don't know. Either way, I bet things weren't going down the way he expected. And, for me, that's one thing I take away from this chapter.

Another point worth pondering is that Joseph's brothers essentially use the same tools to deceive Jacob that he used to deceive his father to steal Esau's birthright: a coat and a goat. So, the same tools were used to trick Esau out of his birthright as were used to steal Joseph's inheritance.

Clearly, there's quite a bit packed into this story, but here's what stuck out the most to me this week: this chapter marks the beginning of a 22-year period before Joseph's dreams were fulfilled. Twenty-two years before he got to see his role in the greatest story ever told. Twenty-two years of servitude, imprisonment, slander, injustice, and just flat-out being forgotten. Then, one day, it all made sense. What humans meant for destruction, God meant for good. The sin of murderous bullies was turned on its head and became the very thing that saved them. On the flip side, the bully brothers also lived out those 22 years before Joseph's dreams came to pass...probably with some shame...but probably often living in the oblivious okayness of life a lot of the time. Then, the opposite side of the equation all became very real to them as well. I bet they remembered the dream. I doubt they knew their story was merely a foreshadowing in the opening chapters of the greatest story ever told...the story all of us humans find ourselves in the midst of. It's a heck of a foreshadowing, too. The one they ridiculed, tormented, and thought they killed became the one with the power to save them. Their guilt, shame, starvation...their journey through a desert of famine...their feeling of utter helplessness...it all culminated as they stood before the one who held the keys to storehouses of more grain than they could ever eat. There they stood, totally at the mercy of the one human who had the power to A) turn them away and let them starve, B) have them all killed immediately; or, C) forgive, redeem, feed, and save them and their entire family.

These brothers got to witness the gospel a couple thousand years before it was written. What they meant for evil, God used for good. Their meaning in the sin was to kill Joseph. God's meaning was to save the killers. And, that's good news for all of us.

AMP up your study of Genesis 37

Apply — Joseph spent 22 years waiting for dreams to be fulfilled that started with him being thrown in a pit. Is there a dream, calling, or promise in your life that you've been waiting on so long you've started to wonder if you misheard? Write it down. Date it. Commit to trusting the story for one more week.

Meditate — Joseph's brothers used the same tools against him that Jacob used against Esau — a coat, a deception, a lie to a father. Generational patterns of sin have a way of showing up wearing familiar clothing. Where do you see a pattern in your own family repeating itself right now? What would it take to interrupt it?

Pray — Pray for someone in your life who is currently in the pit — not because they sinned, but because someone else did. Ask God to remind them that the pit is not the end of the story. Ask for the faith to believe the same thing for yourself if you're the one in the dark right now.

Next week: Genesis Chapter 38 — Ew, Gross

Chapter Thirty-Eight

Week Thirty-Eight: Ew, Gross

Genesis Chapter 38

The night my dad met my mom's parents, they decided to watch a movie together. My dad picked it out. Worried about how they might perceive him based on his movie selection, he prefaced with, "I haven't seen this movie before. I apologize ahead of time if it contains any inappropriate content." My grandma — the lady I've known as the sweetest, kindest soul...the lady who I've always known as one of the purest forms of innocence on this planet — leapt over the couch and exclaimed, "Bring on the sex and violence!"

That seems like a good preface for this passage. Well, it's probably a good preface for quite a few of the Old Testament passages, actually. There's some really messed up stuff in the lineage of our Christ.

Allow me to summarize. Judah fancies an unnamed Canaanite girl. Marriage to Canaanites was frowned upon throughout Israelite history; but he doesn't let that stop him. He has a couple of kids with his Canaanite wife. It doesn't go well, to put it lightly. First, Judah arranges a marriage for his firstborn to a girl named Tamar. Unfortunately, his firstborn, Er, turned out to be a wicked dude and was smited — or is it smote? I'm going with smited — from the face of the earth, leaving Tamar widowed. Based on the fact that she was arrange-married to a guy wicked enough to be smited, she probably wasn't too sad about it. Anyhow, Judah then instructs his other son, Onan, to sleep with Tamar in an effort to carry on the line of Er. Onan does so, but doesn't want to lose a portion of his inheritance, so he, well, he doesn't impregnate her. The Bible is uncomfortably specific about how that works. Thanks, Bible. Onan gets himself smited from the earth as well thanks to this deed. Again, I doubt Tamar was too terribly sad about the loss of Onan. Judah, apparently quite concerned that Tamar is being left without anyone to sleep with, tells her to give it a few years until his next son, Shelah, grows up. It's not looking too promising for ol' Shelah, to be honest. I think Judah perhaps senses this as well and withholds him from Tamar. Tamar resorts to dressing up as a cult prostitute in an effort to have a son and carry on her family line. The plan works far too easily as her father-in-law, Judah, sleeps with her, and she becomes pregnant. Judah finds out and is just happy that his daughter-in-law found love and is having a baby. Just kidding. He orders that she be burned to death. (Let's be honest. Judah is a real piece of work.) Then, in a reveal that would have made Jerry Springer proud, Tamar informs Judah that he is, in fact, the father of her child. He has a solid "Oh, crap." moment, realizes the error of his ways, and declares her more righteous than him. Side note: when you're declaring that a Canaanite woman who pretended to be a cult prostitute in order to sleep with her father-in-law to be more righteous than you, that's a low moment. The Bible then conveniently lets us know that A) Tamar gives birth to twins; and, B) Judah doesn't get the satisfaction of ever sleeping with her again.

That's it. That's the chapter. It's another one of those, "You don't make this stuff up and put it in the Bible if you're creating a non-historical myth or legend about the origin of your people."

So, what's my takeaway this week?

It comes from the unexpected addition of Zerah in the genealogy of Jesus in Matthew 1:3: *"Judah the father of Perez and Zerah, whose mother was Tamar, Perez the father of Hezron, Hezron the father of Ram."*

Interestingly, Zerah is the only non-heir listed in the genealogy of Jesus. So, why does God ensure he is memorialized in Matthew 1:3? Let's look at the last four verses of Genesis 38:

"When the time came for her to give birth, there were twin boys in her womb. As she was giving birth, one of them put out his hand; so the midwife took a scarlet thread and tied it on his wrist and said, 'This one came out first.' But when he drew back his hand, his brother came out, and she said, 'So this is how you have broken out!' And he was named Perez. Then his brother, who had the scarlet thread on his wrist, came out. And he was named Zerah." (Genesis 38:27–30, NIV)

Jesus ultimately comes from the line of Perez, not Zerah. Zerah was the firstborn everyone expected. Perez was the weaker, unexpected heir who broke through — literally and figuratively. The book of Matthew doesn't shy away from the utter sinfulness and brokenness contained in the line of Jesus...which is interesting considering that Matthew is writing down the lineage of his chosen Messiah. Humans tend to want to paint their heroes in as perfect a light as possible. Unless, that is, their hero is the light. Then, there's no need to white-wash or embellish any part of your Messiah's story. You simply tell the truth. So, Matthew confronts the depravity in the lineage of Jesus head on. He straight up calls out the sinfulness in Matthew 1:3 and also in verse 6:

"Judah the father of Perez and Zerah, whose mother was Tamar." (Matthew 1:3, NIV)

"...and Jesse the father of King David. David was the father of Solomon, whose mother had been Uriah's wife." (Matthew 1:6, NIV)

In Matthew 1:6, Matthew mentions that David was the father of Solomon by "the wife of Uriah." He could have simply named Bathsheba; but he wanted the world to remember the brokenness of David as well as the sin of Judah. In Matthew 1:3, he mentions both Perez and Zerah — specifically that their mother was Tamar. He could have simply named Perez and hoped future readers would forget about the whole Tamar and Judah situation; but he wanted the world to remember the brokenness Perez came from. And, that's the story of Genesis 38. It's the story of the Old Testament. It's the story of the New Testament. It's the story of the Bible. Out of the ugliest of sins, the worst of depravities, the most bitter of betrayals, and the emptiness of brokenness comes a most beautiful hope, the best redemption, the sweetness of mercy, and the fullness of justice, forgiveness, and love. Out of the darkness, salvation breaks through.

AMP up your study of Genesis 38

Apply — Matthew didn't hide the brokenness in Jesus's family line —
he put it right at the top of his Gospel. This week, practice the same kind
of honesty. Find one person you trust and tell them something true about
your own story that you usually keep polished or hidden. Not for shock
value — just for the freedom of being known.

Meditate — Perez broke through. The unexpected, weaker one. The
one who wasn't supposed to be first. Where in your own life or family line
has God used the "wrong" person, the broken situation, or the shameful
chapter to produce something beautiful? What does it tell you about the
kind of raw material God prefers to work with?

Pray — Pray for someone you know whose story is a mess right now —
a real, complicated, nobody-would-put-this-in-a-children's-Bible kind of
mess. Ask God to do what he does best: bring Perez out of the chaos. Ask
him to break through in that situation in an unexpected way.

Next week: Genesis Chapter 39 — Joseph's Emotional Rollercoaster

Chapter Thirty-Nine

Week Thirty-Nine: Joseph's Emotional Rollercoaster

Genesis Chapter 39

Back when I was in high school, I watched a movie called *Robin Hood: Men in Tights*. I thought it was hilarious. I tried to watch it again as an adult. Brutal. I turned it off 10 minutes in. But, I digress. In the movie, Robin Hood has a blind friend named Blinkin. I loved that guy. At one point in the movie, blind Blinkin is in the midst of a battle. He is blindly and ridiculously fighting the air with his sword in hopes of walloping an enemy that is nowhere to be seen. Suddenly, Blinkin is hit in the head by something. After being hit in the head, he pauses for a second. You see a look of simultaneous realization and joy emerge on his face as he looks out at the world. He excitedly exclaims, "I CAN SEE!" Almost immediately, he is hit in the head a second time. His face quickly returns to an aloof look, and his hands begin to aimlessly grasp the air in front of him. He dejectedly states, "Nope. I was wrong."

In my life, I've so often felt that "I CAN SEE!"..."Nope. I was wrong" feeling as life seems to be turning a corner for good and justice and peace and joy and happiness...only to have sadness smack me upside the head again. The story of Joseph has resonated with me for that exact reason. I wonder if Joseph felt whipsawed by the rapid shifts from good fortune to bad in his life?

"I've got a lovely coat from my father! Life is good!"

"Nope. I was wrong. I've been left for dead in a cistern."

"I'm in charge of a whole household! Life is better!"

"Nope. I was wrong. I'm back in prison."

Here we are in Genesis 39; and, at first, things seem to be turning around for ol' Joseph. Aside from the fact that he's still pretty much an indentured servant, God is blessing his efforts. Success is around every corner. If I were him, I'd have at least a fleeting thought of, "Finally, the future has hope. Wrongs are beginning to be righted!" Then, like a punch to the gut, Joseph's integrity and "doing the right thing" is rewarded with a false accusation that lands him in prison. In almost an instant, hope for the future turns to fear of being put to death. A glimmer of justice turns to total injustice.

"I CAN SEE!" "Nope. I was wrong."

Personally, I would've experienced some anger and a lot of confusion. Man, oh man...life's a mess just when I thought things were turning around.

Joseph is far from alone. Fortune turns on a dime for quite a few characters in the Bible — especially the quote-unquote "heroes." Take King David for example.

Psalm 21 starts with *"O Lord, in your strength the king rejoices, and in your salvation how greatly he exults! You have given him his heart's desire and have not withheld the request of his lips."* (NIV) This Psalm carries on with similarly gushing joy until it ends in much the same way as it began: *"Be exalted, O Lord, in your strength! We will sing and praise your power."* (NIV)

David is radiating thanks and joy. Then...not so much. I give you literally the next verses in the Bible. Psalm 22:1–2 (NIV):

"My God, my God, why have you forsaken me? Why are you so far from saving me, from the words of my groaning? O my God, I cry by day, but you do not answer, and by night, but I find no rest."

Talk about your all-time mood swings. Can you imagine having this guy in your Bible class at church during prayer request time? That would be uncomfortable. Somebody would definitely be pulling him aside after class. "Um, David, have you considered therapy?" He'd probably be like, "Um, I'm a 'man after God's own heart.' I'm fine. You get a therapist." But, I digress. Oddly, the stories of David and Joseph and others' fortunes turning on a dime encourage me in two big ways.

First, if ever I needed justification that sometimes it's okay to not be okay, the Bible has it. Second, despite the firm beliefs of many to the contrary, sometimes bad things happen to good people — and not because they made a mistake or messed up or even sinned. Sometimes, bad things just happen in a broken world. Of course, sometimes bad things happen to me because I'm an idiot, but it's encouraging that horrible things aren't just "bad karma" for something. That would be a heavy burden to carry.

Those are a couple of my takeaways from Genesis 39. Here's one more, from verses 5 and 6:

"From the time he put him in charge of his household and of all that he owned, the Lord blessed the household of the Egyptian because of Joseph. The blessing of the Lord was on everything Potiphar had, both in the house and in the field. So Potiphar left everything he had in Joseph's care; with Joseph in charge, he did not concern himself with anything except the food he ate." (Genesis 39:5–6, NIV)

Specifically, I want to focus on *"the Lord blessed the household of the Egyptian because of Joseph"* part of those verses.

I think that, too often, we Christians have the opposite effect on those around us. We are not a blessing to those around us. We're more like thorns in society's side than blessings. We've become sort of like societal helicopter parents, ready to swoop in and pronounce judgment when, how, and where judgment is needed. Mostly, we don't act like a servant in prison as Joseph did. We become more like overly righteous imprisoners ready to deal out verbal and online wrath, judgment, and condemnation rather than being a blessing to those around us in a humble, loving, servant type of way. To put it another way, we're more concerned about judging the dirty-ness of people's feet rather than washing them. Even if non-Christians could trust us with their livelihoods as Potiphar trusted Joseph, they certainly wouldn't want to. For me, that's a challenge I'm walking with today — to try to be more known as a humble server of people rather than a self-righteous judger of sinners.

AMP up your study of Genesis 39

Apply — The Lord blessed Potiphar's household *because of Joseph*. Is that true of you? Would the people around you — neighbors, coworkers, friends who don't share your faith — say that their lives are better because you're in them? This week, do one concrete thing to bless someone outside your faith community with no agenda attached.

Meditate — Joseph's integrity cost him his freedom. He did the right thing and went to prison for it. Think of a time when doing the right thing made your life harder, not easier. How did you handle it? What does Joseph's story say about the relationship between faithfulness and immediate reward?

Pray — Pray to be known as a blessing rather than a burden to the people around you. Ask God to make you more like Joseph in Potiphar's house — someone whose presence makes things better, whose work is marked by faithfulness, and whose life points quietly but unmistakably toward God. Then ask for the patience to trust the story even when the prison door closes behind you.

Next week: Genesis Chapter 40 — The Cupbearer and the Baker

Chapter Forty

Week Forty: The Butler and the Baker

Genesis Chapter 40

Poor Joseph is still hanging out in prison. Worth noting: I think there's some significance to the fact that Joseph seems to be the very first Hebrew slave in Egypt. That's some irony for you.

Back to the story. Genesis 40 contains the rather famous story of the butler, the baker, and their prophetic dreams.

Today, I want to talk about the power of empathy and how God often uses it to weave stories together. In Genesis 40, God used Joseph's empathy to further his plans.

Joseph is a guy who has consistently found himself a victim of injustice. Tossed in a well. Sold into slavery. Accused of adultery. Tossed in prison. Yet, you don't sense bitterness and anger towards everyone and everything around him. He doesn't seem to be one of those guys who lets injustice define him. You've met people like that, right? People who have been wronged in this life and just can't let it go? Often, they've been legitimately wronged. It consumes them so much that they become as much a slave to bitterness as they are to injustice. They are very difficult people to be around. They gripe about everything. They sort of just want the world to burn, and they have a difficult time shifting the focus of conversation to anything other than their pain. You feel for them — as much for the fact that they are standing in their own way of progress as for the injustice done to them. Admittedly, I've spent some time as that person. Sorry, world. Perhaps that's why Joseph's question in verse 7 — *"Why do you look so sad today?"* — is such a good reminder for me. If I were in his shoes, there's a decent chance I would have asked the same question, but would have launched into a diatribe about my own problems before the other prisoner had a chance to answer. Whatever his answer, I would've done my best to "one up" him.

"Oh, you poor baker. I'm so sorry that you had a dream that bothered you...but, I didn't even do anything wrong, and I'm stuck here in prison. Potiphar's wife came after me. I just ran away while she stood there holding my dignity. Yet, she's free and happy while I'm rotting away in prison. Where's the justice there?"

To which the baker would have replied, "I know, Josh. You've mentioned it a time or two or three or hundred before."

Of course, Joseph doesn't do that. He genuinely listens. Genuinely answers. Genuinely tries to help. And, that very conversation is the one that eventually propels him out of prison and into power. Emphasis on *eventually*.

Of course, I think empathy works the other way, too. It's easy to get caught up in our own stories so much that we spend our days "one-upping" everybody — good and bad. Again, there's a reminder here for me. Far too often, in my attempt to connect with someone, I redirect the conversation from their accomplishments to my own. I think God likes it better when stories are woven together in a more empathetic, Joseph-like way. There's power in genuine listening. There's power in jumping into someone else's story rather than trying to pull everyone into your own.

Ultimately, that's my takeaway this week: I'm working to do a better job at asking about and empathizing with the lives of those I come into contact with rather than trying to pull them into my story. I'll see where God takes it.

AMP up your study of Genesis 40

Apply — This week, practice one conversation where you ask a question and then just listen — fully, without redirecting to your own story. No one-upping the good news. No one-upping the bad news. Just listen and ask a follow-up question. See what happens when you jump into someone else's story instead of pulling them into yours.

Meditate — Joseph's question — *"Why do you look so sad today?"* — came from a man who had every reason to be consumed by his own pain. What is it about his posture that made space for that question? Where in your life has bitterness or self-focus made it harder to notice what the people around you are carrying?

Pray — Ask God to give you eyes like Joseph this week — eyes that notice the sadness on other people's faces even when your own circumstances are hard. Pray for the grace to be genuinely curious about the lives of the people around you, and for the humility to make them the main character in the conversation.

Next week: Genesis Chapter 41 — To God Goes the Credit

Chapter Forty-One

Week Forty-One: To God Goes the Credit

Genesis Chapter 41

Before we dive in, I want to share a quote that has stayed with me throughout this season of life caring for our son Isaiah:

"Loss creates a barren present, as if one were sailing on a vast sea of nothingness. Those who suffer loss live suspended between a past for which they long and a future for which they hope. They want to return to the harbor of the familiar past and recover what was lost...Or they want to sail on and discover a meaningful future that promises to bring them life again...Instead, they find themselves living in a barren present that is empty of meaning." — Gerald Sittser, *A Grace Disguised*, quoted in John Ortberg, *The Life You've Always Dreamed Of*

Caring for a terminally ill child feels a little like emotional prison sometimes. It's a grief you can't escape. It's a grief that makes it difficult to empathize with the world around me. Each week of this study is a personal challenge for me to hear God's voice — and I hope that God uses it to challenge you in healthy ways as well.

Let's jump into Genesis 41. Here's the first thing that stood out to me: God speaks to people in dreams. To name a few, he spoke to Solomon, Nebuchadnezzar, Moses, Abimelech, Jacob, Laban, Daniel, Pilate's wife, and Joseph in dreams. It seems that God spoke to unbelievers in dreams in the Bible at a ratio of around 2:1...which is interesting. I'll certainly be paying more attention to my dreams.

As is starting to be the painful pattern in his life, Joseph finds himself unjustly forgotten in Genesis 41...and not just for a couple of days. For two years he languishes in prison. Putting myself in Joseph's shoes, I would have found it incredibly difficult to handle this situation as he did. For two years he waited; and, when his moment of opportunity finally arrives, he humbly defers to the power of a God Pharaoh does not believe in. My knee-jerk reaction would have been to use my moment with Pharaoh to argue my case, explain my innocence, and beg for my release. Joseph does none of those things.

"Pharaoh said to Joseph, 'I had a dream, and no one can interpret it. But I have heard it said of you that when you hear a dream you can interpret it.'" (Genesis 41:15, NIV)

What was Joseph's response to Pharaoh in verse 16? He led with this: "Nope. I can't do that..."

Joseph! C'mon, man. Everybody knows when you're hustling, your default answer to whatever is asked of you by anyone in control of your destiny should be, "Yes!"

Hey Joseph, I've heard you can fix the plumbing in my palace. "Of course, yes! I can fix that right up for you. God has gifted me to do so."

Hey Joseph, I need someone to watch my camels for a weekend, can you do that? "Of course, yes! I'm great with camels or lions or cats or whatever animal you need help with!"

Hey Joseph, I've heard you might be able to help me with a PowerPoint presentation I'm giving on how to build a pyramid for dummies. "No problem! I'll work up a template faster than Pharaoh can say, 'Let my people go!'"

Instead, Joseph calmly and confidently makes more of God and less of himself. It's sort of the inverse of the Joseph we saw in Genesis 37 — where we see a father's favorite kid bragging about his fancy robe.

I like to make myself the main character in God's story. I like to be a hero. I like to paint the picture as sort of a "With me alone, a lot of things are possible; but, tack God onto my goals, and all things are possible." That's not the tone of Joseph's discussion with Pharaoh. The tone is clear: "I can't help you. But, God can. I am nothing. God is everything." Joseph is very careful to distinguish the two...even if the consequence had been life and death in prison. Giving God credit is a big deal.

In a nutshell, that's my takeaway this week. The Bible isn't a story about God pointing humanity to a bunch of larger-than-life biblical heroes whom we should all pattern our lives after. The Bible is a story that points us to God. The better we do that for the world around us...the better we point people to God rather than ourselves...the more effective disciples we are.

AMP up your study of Genesis 41

Apply — Think about the last time something went really well in your life — a success, a compliment, a breakthrough. How did you talk about it? Did you give God the credit out loud, or did you quietly absorb it? This week, find one specific opportunity to redirect credit to God in a real conversation — not performatively, but genuinely.

Meditate — Joseph's default was "I can't, but God can." What is your default? When an opportunity arrives that is bigger than your current circumstances, do you lean toward self-promotion or God-promotion? What does your honest answer reveal about who you actually trust?

Pray — Pray the prayer Joseph modeled before Pharaoh: "Not me, God. You." Ask God to make that your instinct — in success, in failure, in moments of visibility, and in moments of obscurity. Ask him to loosen your grip on credit and your need to be seen, and to replace it with the freedom of pointing to him instead.

Next week: Genesis Chapter 42 — A Dream Fulfilled

Chapter Forty-Two

Week Forty-Two: A Dream Fulfilled

Genesis Chapter 42

In Genesis 42, the famine in the land gets bad enough that Joseph's brothers make the trip to Egypt to acquire food.

"But Jacob did not send Benjamin, Joseph's brother, with his brothers, for he feared that harm might happen to him." (Genesis 42:4, NIV)

I don't think Jacob is worried about harm coming to Benjamin from the perils of a hard journey: bumpy roads, wild animals, or bands of thieves. No, I think he's worried about harm coming to Benjamin at the hands of his brothers. Was Benjamin reliving the brotherly jealousy and angst of his brother Joseph? It's possible. Also, I could be wrong, but I'm betting Jacob suspected foul play was involved in Joseph's reported death. I think he either knew or suspected that his boys had lied about the cause of Joseph's death. As a parent, you tend to know when your kids aren't being 100% honest with you. Sometimes, it's easy...like the time I asked my 3-year-old son if he'd eaten a cookie without asking permission. He said, "No," while shaking his head defiantly. His entire face was smeared with chocolate. Terrible liar. Other times, it's not so easy...like those times when something is broken and none of the grade school-aged kids seems to have any idea how it happened. As a parent, you may not be able to figure out the whole truth of a situation; but you know that the story you are being told isn't entirely accurate. I could be wrong, but I think Jacob knew that something horrible had happened to Joseph; and, he wasn't about to let the same thing happen to Benjamin.

Anyhow, we have quite a moment in verse 6. It has been many years and several chapters of background stories; but Joseph's dream from Genesis 37:7 is fulfilled in Genesis 42:6.

Here's one of many instances in the story of Joseph that rings true in my life. Even though I believe wholeheartedly that God fulfills his promises, I'm often completely wrong about the way God accomplishes his plans. Here, Joseph was given a visual picture of what was going to come to pass. And yet, I seriously doubt any part of the story happened as he expected. When his brothers are bowing down to him here in Genesis 42, they do not recognize him. I bet young dreamer Joseph didn't see that coming. Also, Joseph's pathway to a position of power — the position that would induce his brothers to bow down to him — has been anything but great. It wasn't a story of Joseph building a career with his own wisdom or manifesting the life he desired or his parents helping him rise to power or even his brothers slowly coming around over time to realize what a blessing Joseph was to the family. No. None of that. The dream was fulfilled through slavery, injustice, imprisonment, pain, and struggle. And, the very thing most people crave about power — the fame associated with everyone knowing who you are, recognizing your talent, and lauding you for it — all that was missing in the fulfillment of the dream. Again, those bowing down didn't even know his true identity.

To me, Genesis 42 is a reminder that sometimes trusting God means staying faithful no matter what the journey looks like rather than lamenting and whining that things don't look the way you think God should have made them look. Sometimes, being in the center of God's will doesn't mean health, wealth, and success. Sometimes, it means prison, poverty, injustice...even death sometimes. Just because terrible things are happening doesn't mean God isn't moving. Just because terrible things are happening doesn't mean that you are doing something wrong or are even on the wrong path. *And my God will meet all your needs according to the riches of his glory in Christ Jesus."* (Philippians 4:19, NIV) Sometimes, those "glorious riches" aren't money to get you out of a bind, but riches of peace to get you through injustice...riches of energy to get you through a storm.

Of course, sometimes we find ourselves in awful situations because we make idiotic life choices. But, I think it's important to give ourselves a little grace and remember that sometimes, we don't find ourselves in awful situations because of our own choices. Sometimes, we find ourselves in awful situations because it's right where God wants us...and he's on the verge of using you and me to further his story and show the world his greatness in the midst of the worst of life's challenges.

AMP up your study of Genesis 42

Apply — Joseph's dream was fulfilled in a way he never could have predicted — through the exact opposite of what he would have planned. Think about a promise, a calling, or a dream you believe God has placed in your life. Write down the way you expect it to happen. Then spend five minutes genuinely considering that God may fulfill it through a completely different path — and ask yourself if you'd be okay with that.

Meditate — Joseph's brothers bowed before him and didn't even know who he was. The fulfillment of his dream came without the recognition he would have expected. Is there a dream or calling in your life where you've been waiting for the recognition to arrive along with the fulfillment? What would it mean to receive the substance of the promise without the spotlight?

Pray — Pray Philippians 4:19 over your situation this week. Ask God to meet your needs — not necessarily in the way you've asked, but according to his glorious riches. Ask for the faith to trust a God whose fulfillment of promises often looks nothing like what you drew up on the whiteboard.

Next week: Genesis Chapter 43 — Serve the Food

Chapter Forty-Three

Week Forty-Three: Serve the Food

Genesis Chapter 43

For those who haven't followed the story from the beginning, here's a brief recap to bring you up to speed.

God created the world. And, it was good. Then, God created mankind and womankind and placed them in the midst of a garden of all the things they could ever want. In said garden, God gave man and woman one rule: don't eat from that tree over there. If you've ever met humans before, you know exactly how they reacted to the one rule: they broke it. They ate the forbidden fruit and messed up, well, everything. Mankind, womankind, creation, and nature...all of it fractured. All of it broken. But, God had a plan to forgive, redeem, and restore. In the chapters leading up to this one, we've followed the stories of a few of the patriarchs: Abraham, Isaac, and Jacob. We've been seeing a lot of foreshadowing of God's redemption that is to come. In fact, Joseph's story might just be the biggest foreshadowing yet. His family killed him — at least, they thought they did. In doing so, they inadvertently sent him on God's path to a position of power...a position to enact justice or grant mercy.

As things stand in Genesis 43, Joseph's brothers — who have run out of the first supply of food he bestowed upon them — make the nerve-wracking trek back to Egypt to essentially beg for their lives again. Joseph sits at the proverbial right hand of the king with the authority to give life to those who wished him death...or to take their very lives from them.

"When Joseph came home, they presented to him the gifts they had brought into the house, and they bowed down before him to the ground." (Genesis 43:26, NIV)

These sinner brothers who bow in front of the innocent Joseph have messed up. A lot. They hold zero bargaining power. They don't have the resources to buy mercy. They've brought gifts; but let's keep it real. Their gifts are sort of like if I were to give Elon Musk a $20 Starbucks gift card. Also, I realize they don't know Joseph's true identity yet, but they might as well have said, "We sold you and left you for dead; but, hey, here's a Starbucks gift card. Can we have some food so we don't die?" But, I digress. My point: these brothers don't have the resources to buy mercy, and they aren't righteous enough to deserve a favor. They stand powerless hoping against hope for some undeserved grace. Been there, fellas. Solidarity. The choice is Joseph's: enact justified revenge or bestow amazing grace. Enter three of my favorite words in this chapter and in life. *"Serve the food."* (Genesis 43:31)

The sinners were starving, so they ran to the only place — the only one — they knew was capable of feeding them...the only one they knew who was capable of giving them life. These starving fellas threw themselves at the mercy of the one they'd betrayed, and what did he do? Kill 'em all Old Testament judgment and wrath style? No. He had their feet washed (Genesis 43:24, foreshadowing John 13) and was moved with compassion (Genesis 43:30, foreshadowing Matthew 9:36, 14:14, 15:32, 20:34; Mark 1:41; Luke 7:13). Then, Joseph threw those undeserving sinners a feast — introduced with the words we all long to hear in one way or another: *"Serve the food."*

Jesus talked about being the "bread of life." He spoke often of banquets and feasts and food for the hungry. A big part of his ministry was feeding people literally so they would have a taste of what it was like for him to feed them wholly, spiritually.

That's my biggest takeaway from Genesis 43. There are times in all of our lives when we feel as though we're starving. Sometimes, it's because of our own stupid choices. We've lied. We've betrayed. We've sinned. We've fallen short. We desperately want to be rid of that feeling of guilt...that feeling of shame. Starving, we throw up a prayer to the only one we know who has the power to alleviate that guilt and shame...the only one who has the ability to wipe it all away. We have no bargaining chips. We beg for mercy. Do you know what God says in moments like that...when we helplessly bow to his authority and beg for mercy?

"Serve the food."

AMP up your study of Genesis 43

Apply — Think of someone in your life who has wronged you — maybe significantly — who hasn't made it right and may never be able to. This week, pray specifically for one small act of grace you could extend toward them. Not a full reconciliation necessarily. Just one meal's worth of mercy. One "serve the food" moment.

Meditate — The brothers had nothing to offer Joseph. No bargaining chips. No righteousness. No resources sufficient to buy what they needed. They just showed up. When you come to God in prayer, do you come with a list of reasons why you deserve to be heard — your service, your faithfulness, your good behavior? Or do you come like the brothers — empty-handed and desperate? Which posture do you think he actually prefers? Why?

Pray — Come to God this week with empty hands. No list of credentials. No spiritual bargaining chips. Just: *"I'm starving. I have nothing to offer. Feed me."* Then sit quietly and let him serve the food.

Next week: Genesis Chapter 44 — Joseph's Silver Cup

Chapter Forty-Four

Week Forty-Four: The Cup of Divination

Genesis Chapter 44

We've got quite a lot going on here in chapter 44, so let's break it down.

We're toward the end of the ongoing saga of Joseph being reunited with his brothers. In chapter 44, we find Joseph again testing his brothers, this time with a silver cup...and not just any ordinary silver cup.

The brothers have loaded up the grain given to them and have begun the journey back to their father. They're probably feeling pretty good about the trip thus far. No one was executed. They got the grain. They could see the city in their rearview mirror. Phew. Relief.

Then comes Joseph's steward with a journey-stopping, heart-stopping, peace-destroying accusation: someone stole Joseph's silver cup of divination. Not good, guys. Not good.

Let's talk about this cup for a second. First, we have no indication that Joseph ever credited anyone or anything but God with his ability to foresee the years of feast and famine, let alone a cup. However, it wouldn't be much of a stretch to think that many Egyptians — and people who were saved from starvation by the Egyptians — credited their salvation to Joseph's ability to predict the future...and very likely to this particular cup used for divining the future, as it is described in Genesis 44:5.

That said, stealing this particular cup wasn't simply a crime against Joseph but against the kingdom of Egypt as a whole. Stealing a cup from the guy who just saved them was bad. But, stealing *the* cup that held the predictive power to sustain Egypt through a famine...that's very, very bad. No wonder the brothers were distraught when the cup showed up in Benjamin's sack.

"At this, they tore their clothes." (Genesis 44:13, NIV)

Joseph's ability to predict the future had effectively saved the world as they knew it from starvation. In Genesis 44:13, these brothers had the brutal realization that they had somehow A) stolen the possible source of that ability; and, B) angered the guy with all the power.

Of course, it seems that Joseph was testing them to see how they would handle the gravity of the offense. If the cup was in Benjamin's bag, would they do as they had done to Joseph all those years ago? Would they sacrifice Benjamin out of anger or, at best, for the sake of their own lives? Would they drag Benjamin back to Joseph saying, "He took the cup! We had no idea! Kill him and take your cup!" Would they kill Benjamin themselves in an effort to appease Joseph? Or, had they truly changed? I'm sure Joseph was curious how they would handle the situation.

Thankfully, the brothers do appear to have changed. Given the option to rid themselves of another brother who was seemingly more dearly loved by their father, not one of them has the idea to throw Benjamin under the bus. Not one of them suggests murder or abandonment. They could have gone back to Jacob with the story, "I'm sorry. I know you love Benjamin, but he stole from the guy in charge of everything and was executed. There was nothing we could do. His blood is on his own hands." Not this time. In fact, quite the opposite. The brothers refuse to allow Benjamin to pay the price for them. Theologically speaking, we have a bit of substitutionary atonement going on. One of the brothers in particular, Judah, steps up and requests to take the punishment in place of his brother...for the sake of his father. To repeat: we have a guy who didn't commit the crime offer to sacrifice his life for those who did commit the crime, for the sake of his father back home. Of course, that in a nutshell is the gospel. This story is foreshadowing another savior who would come through Judah's lineage.

These were not the same brothers who sold Joseph into slavery all those years ago. Something has changed. No doubt they were still a mess, but we see true guilt, true repentance, and true loyalty to family. They would not sacrifice Benjamin for the sake of their pride, comfort, or inheritance. Instead, they tossed aside all pride, repented, asked for forgiveness, and threw themselves at the mercy of Joseph for the sake of their father. And, as we see in chapter 45, Joseph wept. He saved. He loved. And, he blessed them. That's good news for the brothers. That's good news for us.

AMP up your study of Genesis 44

Apply — The brothers had nothing to offer. No defense. No leverage. They just showed up and threw themselves at Joseph's mercy. Is there a relationship or situation in your life where you've been avoiding that moment — where you know the right thing is to show up empty-handed and ask for forgiveness? It could be something small. It could be something big. Either way, this week, make the call.

Meditate — The brothers had genuinely changed. Twenty-plus years of guilt, consequence, and life had worked something real in them. Think about your own life — where has God used a long, painful season to actually change you, not just chasten you? What is different about you now because of it?

Pray — Thank God for the Judahs in your life — the people who have stepped in and taken a cost that was yours to bear. Then ask God to make you that person for someone else. Ask for the courage to step forward when stepping back would be so much easier.

Next week: Genesis Chapter 45 — Joseph's Big Reveal

Chapter Forty-Five

Week Forty-Five: Joseph's Big Reveal

Genesis Chapter 45

In Genesis 45, we finally arrive at Joseph's big reveal. He can't handle the secrecy anymore and tells his brothers who he really is. They react as expected — standing before their brother in a bit of a dumbfounded and terrified stupor as Joseph explains his rise to a position of power. Joseph also explains that the worst of the famine is yet to come, revealing to his brothers that they are, in fact, only 2 years into a 7-year famine.

Of course, chapter 45 of Genesis serves as a big reveal in a couple of ways: first to Joseph's brothers, and second to all of us who've read the New Testament. There's heavy foreshadowing of Christ here. The son whom the nations of Israel ridiculed, killed, and cast aside rose to power. Then, the son saved them all. But, he didn't just save them all. He gave them the best of the land of the kingdom as well as sustenance to survive the hardest of times on this earth.

Throughout the book of Genesis, the children of Israel find themselves in situations they are unable to work their way out of. In fact, no matter how hard they would have worked to preserve their inheritance, famine would have wiped it all away...and, it would have wiped them away, too. But, grace prevailed.

Joseph gave them life and preserved their inheritance. Perhaps it is better stated this way: the brothers believed they had taken away life and inheritance by an act of ultimate betrayal. Joseph gave them life and inheritance in an act of ultimate grace and forgiveness. It is also worth noting that Joseph reveals himself to his brothers at their second coming — foreshadowing a Messiah who will reveal himself to the world at his second coming.

Back to Genesis 45. Jacob didn't believe his sons when they shared the news of Joseph's survival and rise to power. I imagine that was quite a difficult conversation.

Brothers: "Great news, dad! Joseph is alive and is now ruler over all the land of Egypt! He is giving us land, food, and supplies to sustain us through the famine. We're saved!"

Jacob: "Um, I thought you said he was killed by wild animals?"

Brothers: "Well, dad, um, about that... Um...I think it's important to remember that we might all be dying of starvation right now if not for what happened all those years ago..."

Verse 24 tells me that Joseph saw this stress coming: *"Then he sent his brothers away, and as they departed, he said to them, 'Do not quarrel on the way.'"* (Genesis 45:24, ESV)

For the remainder of the chapter, the brothers — these deceivers, liars, betrayers, and murderers — relay good news to their father. In a way, they relay *the* good news to their father. What they meant for evil, God meant for good.

"So, dad. Here's the thing. We sinned. We really, really messed up. We killed the son you loved. We've carried around secrets and guilt and shame for most of our lives. You can imagine our surprise when the one person we sinned the most against — the one who had every right and reason to want us punished — revealed to us that he alone had the power to give us life or to take it. He could have (and probably should have) executed us on the spot; or, he could have let us march back here and starve to death. But, here's the deal, dad. He wants to save us. All of us. Not only did he choose to spare our lives, he is giving us the best of the land and providing for us throughout the rest of this famine...and the rest of our lives. He was imprisoned when we should have been. He was punished when we should have been. Where there should be animosity, there is grace. Where there should be sadness, there is joy. Where there should be imprisonment, there is freedom. Where there should be death, there is life."

That's good news.

"And they told him, 'Joseph is still alive, and he is ruler over all the land of Egypt.' And his heart became numb, for he did not believe them." (Genesis 45:26, ESV)

Numb. Calloused. Dismissive. This messed up world sure wants to make our hearts that way. Numb to the possibility of good news...or the possibility that we need good news. Maybe we're pretty great after all. Perhaps we don't need salvation. Or, if we do, maybe we can just work our way out of this famine-filled life. Just a few more self-help books. Just a couple million dollars. Just the right career path. Just the right spouse. Then, we'll have inner peace and joy. We don't need a savior. We just need to save ourselves.

May my heart not become numb lest I not believe good news either...because here's a core belief of mine: I feel the weight of a debt I cannot pay. I need salvation, but I'm incapable of attaining it on my own. And, that's ok...because someone else paid the price for me. The less my heart is numb to that, the more grace, peace, and joy I feel. The more numb my heart is to that, the less grace, peace, and joy I feel. The path through suffering is not to callous the heart or to numb yourself to the potential of good news. Neither is it white-knuckled self-betterment, career advancement, or doing of good deeds to put your con-science at ease. No, the path through suffering is the acceptance of the good news that my salvation doesn't depend on me. It depends on one who has already paid the price.

I'll close with these two verses:

"And now do not be distressed or angry with yourselves because you sold me here, for God sent me before you to preserve life." (Genesis 45:5, ESV)

"The thief comes only to steal and kill and destroy. I came that they may have life and have it abundantly." (John 10:10, ESV)

AMP up your study of Genesis 45

Apply — Jacob's heart was numb — too calloused by loss and disappointment to believe good news when it arrived. Is your heart numb to anything right now? Pick one promise from Scripture this week and read it out loud every morning, not as a formality but as a deliberate act of softening. Let the good news land.

Meditate — Joseph said to his brothers, *"Do not quarrel on the way."* He knew the reunion ahead would be complicated and that guilt and blame would be tempting travel companions. What quarrel are you carrying into a situation that God is trying to bring restoration to? What would it look like to lay it down before you arrive?

Pray — Pray the words of Genesis 45:5 over a painful chapter in your own life: *"God sent me before you to preserve life."* Ask God to help you see his redemptive purpose in the hardest thing that has happened to you. Ask for the faith to believe that what others meant for harm, he is using for good.

Next week: Genesis Chapter 46 — How God Weaves Stories Together

Chapter Forty-Six

Week Forty-Six: How God Weaves Stories Together

Genesis Chapter 46

One of the most striking visual representations of the Bible's internal coherence is a data visualization created by designer Chris Harrison, which maps all the cross-references in Scripture — thousands of arcs connecting passages across the Old and New Testaments. It's a powerful image of just how thoroughly God has woven this story together across time.[1] (Check out the link in the footnotes or on my Genesis 46 post at joshwoodtx.substack.com.) Genesis 46 is a small but beautiful example of that weaving.

Here's a quick three-sentence recap of the story of Joseph: the favored son was rejected by his family, thought to be dead, but found to be alive — and has now brought salvation to his family. In short, we've seen the gospel message play out in the Old Testament.

In Genesis 46, all 70 members of Jacob's family head to Egypt. Joseph can't wait until they make it to him, so he runs to meet them in Goshen where, at long last, he sees his father again.

"Joseph had his chariot made ready and went to Goshen to meet his father Israel. As soon as Joseph appeared before him, he threw his arms around his father and wept for a long time." (Genesis 46:29, NIV)

Interestingly, we see the exact phrase "threw his arms around" four times in the Bible. In Genesis 33 when Esau embraces Jacob as they reunite as adults, he "threw his arms around him." In Genesis 45 when Joseph embraces his brother Benjamin, he "threw his arms around him." Here in Genesis 46, Joseph threw his arms around his father. The words appear again in the story of the prodigal son in the New Testament:

"But while he was still a long way off, his father saw him and was filled with compassion for him; he ran to his son, threw his arms around him and kissed him." (Luke 15:20, NIV)

When the Bible repeats the same phrases across decades and centuries and across the Old and New Testaments, I don't think it's a coincidence.

Last year, I went through a study on the book of Genesis that approached it not as divinely inspired Scripture but as a remarkable piece of ancient literature — dissecting its themes from an academic, literary perspective rather than a spiritual one. The author wasn't a Christian and believed some parts to be myth and others to be historic. Yet, among the few clues as to his belief system was a comment that the book of Genesis was so well-written and so well-organized from a literary perspective that he believed it to be divinely inspired. I appreciated that he held the book in such high regard. I also enjoyed looking at Genesis from another angle. It helped me place myself in the stories as a spectator rather than falling into my usual temptation — which is to dissect every word I read as if I were writing a master's-level thesis on it. I mean, I suppose it's great to do that sort of thing, but it's sometimes equally great to simply read, enjoy, and immerse yourself in the story. Reading this way helped me do exactly that as I read through Genesis 46 and Luke 15 — to empathize with the characters, visualize the setting, feel the tension, see the sights, smell the smells, hear the sounds. As a side note: as recorded in the gospel of Luke, it takes Jesus fewer than 500 words — fewer words than this chapter — to paint one of the most memorable stories of all time.

I think both authors — the author of Genesis and the author of Luke — were divinely inspired to use the same wording to draw us into the stories. By literary design, you feel the tension of Joseph. This is a moment he has waited a brutal lifetime for. He's waited through years of betrayal and slavery and injustice and imprisonment and pain for this reunion. For years, he has probably dreamt of this moment — not in a prophetic way but in a "I can't wait to see my dad again someday" way. He can't help but run to Goshen, throw his arms around his father, and weep. There's a whole massive story of grace in that embrace. He forgave and saved his brothers when he could have sentenced them to death. In addition to the joyous reunion of a father and son, every person in Jacob's family was, in this moment, beginning a new life when they should have been continuing along a barren road to death. Jacob knew it. Joseph knew it. Everyone knew it. Joy. Pure joy broke out.

The prodigal son story in the New Testament feels very similar but with a reversal of roles. In the story of the prodigal son, the father throws his arms around his son rather than the son throwing his arms around the father. In both cases, the giver of grace rather than the receiver of grace begins the embrace — which is notable. In both stories, there's a whole massive story of grace in that embrace. The giver has waited through years of betrayal and injustice and pain. These stories resonate even outside of Christian or religious circles. Why? Because they stoke emotions engrained in every human being. If and when a father-and-son relationship is broken, we desperately want it fixed. We long for restoration. Whether we're 10-year-old kids who lied to our parents about eating candy, or 16-year-old kids who accidentally wrecked our parents' car, or 40-year-old kids who handled an argument poorly — the thought of a father throwing his arms around us and saying, "It's ok, son, I love you!"...well...it's powerful. And, it's pointing us to something even greater: an even greater restoration, an even greater grace, an even greater joy.

I think that's what this reunion in Genesis 46 is telling us — and the reunion in Luke 15, for that matter: a reunion with a loving father, the embrace of grace we all long for...it's there waiting for each and every one of us. We just have to accept it.

Here's one more interesting thread woven through this chapter. If you've read the Bible, you've picked up on the fact that a few numbers are used repeatedly: 3, 7, 12, 40, 70, and others. The repeated use of certain numbers made stories easier to remember and retell — particularly helpful for societies that relied on oral tradition. Add symbolism to each number and the stories become even more memorable. For example, do you remember how long the Israelites wandered in the desert? If you know your biblical numerology, you would guess 40 years — because 40 typically represents trial or testing. Conversely, if someone told you the Israelites spent 40 years in the desert, you'd understand that meant a period of testing and/or punishment. Numbers add weight to stories.

Here in Genesis 46, we see the number 70. Seventy members of Jacob's clan went to Egypt to begin the Hebrews' exile. The number 70 typically represents wholeness or completion — God united with mankind, whole and complete. The fact that 70 members of Jacob's clan went to Egypt suggests a harmonic complete unit of people, marching forward with God for his intended purpose.

Fast forward to the New Testament. In the gospel of Luke, Jesus sends out 70 disciples. These disciples would return to the land of exile to share the good news. In Genesis 46, God reveals the good news to his people that they have been saved, unites with them, and they march together into the darkness of Egypt to fulfill his divine plan. In Luke 10, God unites with his people and marches into the world to give everyone the good news that they have been saved.

In Genesis, the son saves the family by bringing them out of their land and into the land of the pagans. In Luke, the father saves the world by again sending his family into the land of the pagans. That's quite a theme — woven together in multiple ways across hundreds of pages of Scripture written by multiple authors of different ethnicities over the course of thousands of years. That's powerful. That's memorable. That's divine.

[1] Chris Harrison, "Bible Cross-References Visualization," chrisharrison.net/index.php/visualizations/BibleViz.

AMP up your study of Genesis 46

Apply — Read the parable of the prodigal son this week (Luke 15:11–32) and the reunion of Joseph and Jacob (Genesis 46:28–30) back to back. Sit with the parallels. Then ask yourself: which character in each story do you most identify with right now — the one running home, the one waiting, or the one watching from a distance?

Meditate — "Threw his arms around him." Four times in the Bible, across thousands of years of history, God uses the same phrase to describe the same moment: grace running toward the guilty. How does it feel to know that the God of the universe runs toward you? That he doesn't wait for you to compose yourself before he embraces you?

Pray — If you've been living like the prodigal — distant from God, self-sufficient, feeding on husks — come home this week. Literally pray the words, *"Father, I am coming home."* If you've been waiting and watching like the father, pray for the one who is still a long way off. Ask God to help you see them coming while they're still far off — and to run.

Next week: Genesis Chapter 47 — God With Us

Chapter Forty-Seven

Week Forty-Seven: God With Us

Genesis Chapter 47

Genesis 47 is a rather interesting chapter — especially if you're familiar with the story of the Israelites' Exodus from Egypt and the familiar words, *"Let my people go!"*

Genesis 47 is essentially the prelude to *"Let my people go!"* Ironically, this prelude is basically, *"Let my people come and stay."* As you may recall from Genesis 15, Abraham had a vision about this very thing happening. In fact, the length of the Israelites' stay in Egypt is foretold: 400 years.

"As the sun was setting, Abram fell into a deep sleep, and a thick and dreadful darkness came over him. Then the Lord said to him, 'Know for certain that for four hundred years your descendants will be strangers in a country not their own and that they will be enslaved and mistreated there.'" (Genesis 15:12–13, NIV)

Throughout the Bible, Egypt is symbolic of a place of sin, oppression, and struggle. This keeps with the Old Testament theme that many things are physical representations of spiritual realities. To me, here's one of the important messages of Israel's time in Egypt — the forthcoming 400-year period that begins in chapter 47 of Genesis and ends with one of the greatest stories of liberation ever told. In this life, God's people will inevitably spend time in the land of Egypt, metaphorically speaking. We will find ourselves in a land of injustice, darkness, pain, frustration, and toil. God's people will suffer. We will struggle. We will hurt. We will cry. But, even in the midst of our sojourn in that land — in the midst of this time when we are strangers in a country not our own, when we will be enslaved and oppressed and struggling mightily — God shows up.

Here's what he shows us through the nation of Israel: even in the tough times, God steps in and gives his people a place to live despite their displacement, food and provision despite famine, employment despite economic peril, increased possessions despite hardship, and increased numbers despite their predicament.

When speaking of suffering and trials, Jesus doesn't talk about avoiding, transcending, or overcoming them by work ethic or sheer will. He talks about sustenance in the valleys, not avoiding the valleys altogether. He talks about walking through our trials with us. With us through the fires. With us through the seas. With us through the deserts. With us through the wildernesses. With us through the valleys. With us through the storms.

"...and they will call him Immanuel (which means 'God with us')." (Matthew 1:23, NIV)

One day, true freedom will come. That's the promise of Christianity. A promise that began when God walked through the sacrifice in Genesis 15, and has been reiterated across every generation. As Tim Keller put it — with a hat tip to J.R. Tolkien — *"Everything sad is going to come untrue and it will somehow be greater for having once been broken and lost."*

Until then — until the time when all the wrongs on earth are righted — we can count on God being with us in our times of famine, oppression, fear, and pain.

Speaking personally, we've spent years in a proverbial desert. We've spent years watching our wonderful son digress from running, dancing, playing, and happily talking our ears off, to brutally losing each and every one of those abilities. As of this writing, our boy is unable to move or communicate due to a constant barrage of seizures and struggle. On a good day, he has 10–20 seizures.

On a good day, he can very sporadically communicate with us via his eyes and "yes" and "no" cards we hold up to his left and right — he shifts his eyes to his answer. Unfortunately, this work of communicating often causes seizures, keeping communication extremely limited. On a bad day, he has 50–100 seizures. On those days, our hours are filled with pure torture. I wish there were another way to describe it, but I can't think of a more adequate word for holding your son as he seizes, turns blue, and struggles not to drown in his own saliva...again, and again, and again. It's unimaginable and indescribable suffering.

As my wife and I have trudged through our own valley of the shadow of death, we have wrestled with the toughest questions life has to offer — questions of faith and doubt, religion and belief, hope and despair. And, as we sat at the end of our proverbial rope, we had a moment where we sort of looked at each other and said something to the effect of, "We've cried, yelled, fought, and wrestled with religion and God. Torture or no torture, we actually believe this Jesus stuff. The Bible is true. All of it. It must be; because in the midst of the worst kind of pain I could possibly fathom, we've found those old biblical promises to be true in our life. There's peace that passes understanding. There's strength when we shouldn't have any. There is hope when we shouldn't have any. There are moments of joy and anticipation when there should be nothing but pain and resignation. We have felt God with us in a very real way."

Does belief in the God of the Bible make it easy to live a life packed with suffering? Did it make it easy for the Israelites to live enslaved? No. We trudge through life as I imagine the Israelites did. Sometimes a week at a time. Sometimes a day at a time. Sometimes a minute at a time. I imagine they replayed God's promises in their minds over and over again just as we do today. There are no promises of a struggle-free life, only a promise that suffering has an end date. And, that peace, joy, resurrection, justice, satisfaction, and perfection will one day come. May it come quickly.

"I have told you these things, so that in me you may have peace. In this world you will have trouble. But take heart! I have overcome the world." (John 16:33, NIV)

AMP up your study of Genesis 47

Apply — Egypt was a hard place, but God provided inside it. This week, identify one specific way God has provided for you inside your own "Egypt" — the hard season, the painful circumstance, the place you never wanted to be. Write it down. Tell someone about it. Let the provision be known.

Meditate — Emmanuel: God with us. Not God above us, watching. Not God ahead of us, waiting. With us. In the ICU. In the desert. In the prison. In the famine. Where in your life have you most clearly felt the *with-ness* of God? And where right now do you most need to believe it?

Pray — Pray John 16:33 out loud this week: *"In this world you will have trouble. But take heart! I have overcome the world."* Pray it for yourself. Pray it for someone you love who is in their own Egypt right now. Let the overcomer speak into the overwhelmed.

Next week: Genesis Chapter 48 — Jacob Blesses Joseph's Sons

Chapter Forty-Eight

Week Forty-Eight: Bypassing the Older for the Sake of the Younger

Genesis Chapter 48

As Jacob nears the end of his life, he calls in Joseph's boys, Ephraim and Manasseh, to bless them before he dies. Joseph brings his sons before his father, placing Manasseh, the older, on Jacob's right and the younger, Ephraim, on Jacob's left. Joseph's intention was for the oldest to receive the greater blessing as was the custom. However, Jacob crosses his hands and gives the greater blessing to the younger, Ephraim. This keeps the pattern we've seen play out several times already, including with Jacob himself — the younger usurps the older in blessing and honor.

God accepted Abel's offering over Cain's in Genesis 4. Isaac was chosen over his older brother, Ishmael. God chose Jacob as the father of the 12 tribes of Israel rather than Jacob's older brother, Esau. Perez "broke out" in front of his brother Zerah. Joseph — who spent his childhood as the youngest sibling — was chosen by God to lead and save his people and the nation of Israel. Aaron was three years older than Moses, but God chose Moses to lead the Israelites out of Egypt. God chose Gideon, the youngest in his family, to deliver Israel from the Midianites. God chose David to be king rather than any of his seven older brothers. God chose David's son Solomon to be king instead of his older brothers.

As I discussed back in chapter 21, the pattern of the Bible isn't just younger usurping the older. It's weak made strong. It's *the last shall be first and the first shall be last.*

Moses — a stutterer — leads the peace negotiation talks with Pharaoh. Gideon — the weakest member of the weakest tribe — leads God's army. Jacob — not only younger, but a deceiver, a manipulator, and a liar. Paul — a mass-murderer of Christians — becomes the author of much of the New Testament.

The Bible is full of people like this. Abraham was old. Elijah was suicidal. Joseph was abused. Job went bankrupt. Moses had a speech problem. Gideon was afraid. Samson was a womanizer. Rahab was a prostitute. The Samaritan woman was divorced. Noah was a drunk. Jeremiah was young. Jacob was a cheater. David was a murderer. Jonah ran from God. Peter denied Christ three times. Martha worried about everything.

Most importantly, the son of a teenage mom and carpenter dad from podunkville, Israel proves himself to be the savior of the world.

"So the last will be first, and the first will be last." (Matthew 20:16, NIV)

"But he said to me, 'My grace is sufficient for you, for my power is made perfect in weakness.' Therefore I will boast all the more gladly about my weaknesses, so that Christ's power may rest on me. That is why, for Christ's sake, I delight in weaknesses, in insults, in hardships, in persecutions, in difficulties. For when I am weak, then I am strong." (2 Corinthians 12:9–10, NIV)

One more note before we leave Genesis 48: the blessing Jacob gave to Joseph's boys was quite an act of faith — both on the part of Jacob and the part of Joseph. Here they were at the very beginning of the nation's sojourn in Egypt, and Jacob was blessing future generations with land that had been promised by God...land they did not currently inhabit. Joseph — by way of his sons — was accepting the blessing, believing in the future land, people, and nation of Israel.

Why is all of this good news for you and me, thousands of years later? Because God blesses the weak. Congrats — we're weak. We're the weaker, deceiver, sinner, outcast, etc. God chose to bless each and every one of us anyway. The strong was sacrificed for the sake of the weak...so that the weak might become strong. I think that's why the pattern is reiterated throughout the Bible — to show us that, no matter how weak and sinful we are, there is hope for us. There is promise for us. I don't know what your particular sin is, but I'm guessing you didn't toss your brother in a well and leave him for dead. I'm guessing you didn't slaughter an entire city for defiling your sister. I'm guessing you didn't use your position of authority to sleep with someone's wife and then have that someone killed to hide your sin. If God's blessing passed through all those messed up people in the Bible, it passes in and through you and me as well. That's good news.

AMP up your study of Genesis 48

Apply — Look at that list of flawed people God used — the drunk, the stutterer, the murderer, the prostitute, the worrier, the runaway. Find the one that most closely matches your own story or your own struggle. Write their name down. Then write down what God did through them anyway. Let it be a promise for your own life this week.

Meditate — Jacob's blessing skipped the firstborn — again. He crossed his hands deliberately, intentionally choosing the unexpected one. Where in your life have you been overlooked, passed over, or treated as the lesser? What would it mean to believe that God's hands are crossed over you — that He has intentionally chosen you, in spite of and because of your weakness?

Pray — Pray 2 Corinthians 12:9–10 over your life this week. Name your specific weakness — out loud, to God. Then ask him to make his power perfect in exactly that place. Ask for the grace to stop hiding your weakness and start offering it to God as the very thing he wants to work through.

Next week: Genesis Chapter 49 — The Scepter Shall Not Depart

Chapter Forty-Nine

Week Forty-Nine: The Scepter Shall Not Depart

Genesis Chapter 49

We are officially one chapter away from the end of the book of Genesis. Thus far, we've already seen the best and worst of humanity...mostly the worst. In fact, though God's people have yet to receive the 10 Commandments, they've done a remarkable job breaking them in spectacularly abhorrent ways. Here in Genesis 49, we see some immediate and generational consequences of the terrible sins of God's chosen people as Jacob blesses his sons. Well, at least the heading in most Bibles over this chapter is "Jacob Blesses His Sons." I'm not so sure you could call a lot of these words "blessings." I mean, Jacob leads off with, "Reuben, you've excelled thus far in life; but you won't any more because you slept with my concubine. Your future is going to be bad now. Real bad. Simeon and Levi, you know how our culture values family togetherness and love? Well, those things will evade you on account of your rage issues — i.e., that time you tricked an entire city into getting circumcised and then murdered them all." After the pronouncement of these "blessings," I'm sure at least a couple of the sons were left standing there wide-eyed saying, "Wait, what? That's it? That's my blessing? Ah, c'mon!"

Though the Bible zooms in and out on various stories of the descendants of each of these sons, it's pretty clear that what we've seen thus far in the book of Genesis sets the tone for the rest of the Bible. People do horrible things again and again and again. When the people turn away from God and follow their own impulses and desires, things get awful fast. When the people turn away from their own impulses and turn toward God, things get better.

If you grew up in church or spent much time in one, you've very likely heard the phrase, "You can't out-sin the grace of God." I suppose that's one rather succinct way to sum up the Old Testament. Time and again God engages his people. Time and again God rescues them. In the book of Genesis alone, we see opportunities in every generation for God to break his original promise. There are times when God could have simply let someone die — or not let someone be born — and the line of Jesus left severed and broken. Yet, here at the end of the book of Genesis, a father is reunited with his sons — ironically, thanks to the one they all cast aside and left for dead. Does that mean that they all live happily ever after? Unfortunately, no. Some will choose a path of relationship, repentance, submission, faith, and family. Some will choose to follow after things and money and women and stuff. Some will straight up choose violence.

Here's something new I learned as I studied Genesis 49 this week. It has to do with Genesis 49:10: *"The scepter will not depart from Judah."* (NIV) Even through captivity and even under foreign rule, a prince of Judah remained head over the tribes of Israel. Then, in A.D. 7, while under Herod and Roman rule, Israel lost the last semblance of self-governance.

At the time, the rabbis considered it a disaster of unfulfilled Scripture. Seemingly, the last vestige of the scepter had passed from Judah, and they did not see the Messiah. Reportedly, rabbis walked the streets of Jerusalem and said, *"Woe unto us, for the scepter has been taken away from Judah, and Shiloh has not come."* — Shiloh being a Jewish idiom for Messiah.[1]

Of course, Christians believe that the Genesis 49:10 prophecy was forever fulfilled in Jesus. Interestingly, at the exact moment in history it seemed that the scepter had departed from Judah, the scepter had passed to Jesus. He was beginning his rule of perfect servant leadership, perfect sacrifice, and perfect fulfillment of Genesis 49:10...and every other biblical promise. Just when rabbis had taken to the streets to lament that all was lost, all things were being made new.

And, that's one of the ultimate graces of Christianity. Just when life feels that way — pointless, meaningless, hopeless — just when you're feeling that all is lost...just when you're feeling that there is no way out, God is near and working in the background. In short, when you're at rock bottom, we have hope. It may feel like Friday; but Sunday is coming.

[1] *Kol HaTor, "Shilo: Jewish Sources and Interpretation of Shiloh," kolhator.com; David Guzik, "Study Guide for Genesis 49," Blue Letter Bible, blueletterbible.org.*

AMP up your study of Genesis 49

Apply — "You can't out-sin the grace of God." Is there something in your past — or your present — that you've quietly decided puts you outside the reach of that statement? This week, bring it specifically to God. Not in a general "forgive me for my sins" way, but by name. Let the grace of the cross meet the specific thing you've been carrying.

Meditate — The rabbis were walking the streets lamenting that all was lost — at the exact moment in history the Messiah was being born. Think about a season of your life when it felt like the scepter had departed — when all seemed lost or God seemed absent. Looking back, what was God doing in the background that you couldn't see at the time?

Pray — Pray for someone in your life who is in their own "Friday" right now — convinced that all is lost, that the scepter has departed, that the Messiah isn't coming. Pray specifically that God would give them the faith to hold on until Sunday. Then pray the same for yourself.

Next week: Genesis Chapter 50 — The End of the Beginning

Chapter Fifty

Week Fifty: The End of the Beginning

Genesis Chapter 50

As we close out the book of Genesis, let's discuss Joseph as a type of Christ. First, let's discuss the origin of the word "type." Why? Primarily because it's my Genesis study and I find it interesting — in spite of the fact that most of humanity probably does not. Anyhow, the word "type" means a person or thing symbolizing or exemplifying the ideal or defining characteristics of something. So, why do we call the action of pressing buttons on a computer keyboard "typing"?

I'm glad you asked.

Back in the day, skilled laborers would carve letters or characters onto the surfaces of blocks of metal or wood. These blocks were used in the printing process. Ink would transfer from the carved letter onto paper. So, the ink represented a "type" of the carved letter in that it wasn't the particular letter itself, but it was a serviceable copy — a "type" of the letter. There's your semi-useless information for the day. You're welcome.

Throughout the Bible, we see "types" of the coming Messiah, Jesus. In fact, every story in the Bible points to Jesus in some way. The Old Testament foreshadows a savior who is to come. The New Testament talks about his coming. The Old Testament "types" of Jesus aren't carbon copies so much as they provide hints and insight into the one to come. For example, throughout the Old Testament, the Hebrew people are ruled by various authorities. For a time, they are ruled by the patriarchs. For a time, by priests. For a time, by prophets. For a time, by judges. For a time, by kings. During each period, they got a taste of what life would be like to be ruled by a good prophet, a good priest, a good king, a good judge, and a good father. But, it was just a taste...a shadow of what was to come. And, they longed for one who would not be just a shadow but the full goodness of all those authorities rolled up into one. A good and perfect father. A good and perfect king. A good and perfect judge. A good and perfect priest.

Back to Joseph. Joseph was a type, a shadow, and a foreshadowing of who the coming Christ would be and what his salvation would look like. Let's look at some of the parallels.

They are both described as shepherds. They both give hope and food to sustain people during hard times. They are both betrayed for the price of a slave. They are both the firstborn of their mothers. They are both dearly loved by their fathers. They are both sent on an errand by their fathers. There were dreams and prophecies about what both of them were going to do. They both began their ministries at age 30. They were both falsely accused. They both avoid temptation. They are both put into a prison or tomb. They both delivered their people after a hard experience. They were both stripped of their garments before being cast down. They both delivered their people as well as those who weren't their people. They were both unknown and unrecognized by those they came to save. They both had the choice to grant grace or to punish by death. They are both thought to be dead and powerless but are found to be alive with authority and power. They both rose from a pit to a position of power. Joseph asked to be remembered by a cupbearer. Jesus asked to be remembered by cupbearers: *"Do this in remembrance of me."*

For all of those reasons and more, the Joseph story is a perfect ending to a book about beginnings. It sets the stage for Old Testament stories being physical representations of spiritual realities. It reminds the world that, when it feels as though all is lost...when it feels as though hope is gone...when it feels as though life is doomed to misery...when it feels as though we've reached the end, the story of Joseph reminds us it's only just the beginning. The beginning of grace and mercy and salvation and peace and justice and joy. A new creation. A Genesis.

AMP up your study of Genesis 50

Apply — You've made it through fifty chapters of the greatest story ever told. Don't let it end here. Pick one theme, one person, or one chapter from this year's study that stayed with you most — and find one practical way to carry it forward into your daily life. Write it down. Share it with someone. Let the study produce something in you that outlasts the reading.

Meditate — Joseph is a type of Christ. The entire book of Genesis — from the first word to the last — is pointing to Jesus. Looking back across the fifty chapters you've just walked through, where do you see that thread most clearly? What aspect of the character of God do you understand more deeply now than you did at the beginning?

Pray — Thank God for the year. Thank him for the hard chapters and the confusing ones, for the stories that made you laugh and the ones that stopped you cold. Ask him to continue the work he began in you through this study. And ask for the faith of the patriarchs — not the faith that never doubted, but the faith that kept walking anyway.

Conclusion

Reflecting on Genesis

Well. We made it.

Fifty chapters. Fifty weeks. One year in the book of beginnings.

I'll be honest with you — when I started this study, I wasn't entirely sure I'd finish it. Not because I didn't love Genesis, but because life has a way of making even the best intentions feel ambitious. If you've followed along from the beginning, you know that a significant portion of this study was written in fits and starts, in hospital rooms and sleepless nights, in the margins of a life that has been anything but neat and tidy. That's probably why I titled this whole thing *Amidst the Chaos* in the first place.

But here we are.

And here's what I keep coming back to as I reflect on a year in Genesis: the chaos was always part of the story.

Adam and Eve didn't get a smooth start. Neither did Noah, or Abraham, or Isaac, or Jacob, or Joseph. Not one of the people God chose to carry his story forward had a clean, orderly, well-planned life. They had famines and feuds and betrayals and grief and bad impulse decisions and seasons of silence from God that stretched on far longer than anyone would have chosen. They had moments of breathtaking faith and moments of breathtaking stupidity — sometimes in the same chapter. And yet, God's story moved forward. Through every mess, through every detour, through every cistern and prison and season of waiting, the story kept moving.

I think that's certainly among the most important things I've taken from this year in Genesis: God doesn't need ideal conditions to work. He doesn't need you to have it together. He doesn't need a clean house, a steady pulse, or a five-year plan. He just needs you to keep walking with him. Enoch walked with God. That's the whole résumé. Three words. And God took him away. Alive.

I also can't leave this book without saying something about what it's like to study the Bible when life is at its hardest.

There is a temptation, when you're in the middle of real suffering, to treat the Bible as a vending machine — to punch in your prayer and wait for the relief to dispense. And when it doesn't, the temptation is to decide that the machine is broken, or that it was never really stocked in the first place. I've been there. My wife has been there. If you're honest, you've probably been there too.

What I've found — not as a theological argument but as a lived experience — is that the Bible isn't a vending machine. It's more like a companion. It doesn't always give you what you asked for, but it sits with you in the dark. It shows you that the darkness has a name, that it has been survived before, and that it has an expiration date. The hovering always ends. God always speaks. Light always comes. Not always on our timeline. Not always in the form we expected. But it comes.

As of this writing, my son Isaiah continues his fight. Our days still look nothing like what we planned. The oxygen alarm still goes off at unexpected hours. The seizures still come. The chaos is still very much amidst us. And yet, in the middle of all of it, I have found something I needed to remember...something I needed to rediscover. I found that the ancient stories of Genesis are not ancient at all. They are alive. They breathe. They meet you exactly where you are.

When I read about Jacob wrestling in the dark, I know that feeling.

When I read about Joseph in the pit, wondering if the dreams were wrong, I know that feeling.

When I read about Abraham staring at the stars and asking God, *How can I know?* — I know that feeling.

And when I read about a God who walked through the blood covenant so that his people wouldn't have to, who brought people from a pit to a palace, who met people in the midst of their mess — I know that feeling too. Or at least, I'm learning to.

That's the invitation of Genesis. Not to have all the answers. Not to resolve every tension or explain every bizarre story or defend every difficult passage. The invitation is simply to walk with a God who has been faithful from the very first word — and to trust that the story he is telling through your life, however chaotic and unfinished it may feel, is pointing somewhere glorious.

It is not good for man to be alone.

Walk with God.

Don't love money and use people. Love people and use money.

What man meant for evil, God meant for good.

Come and see.

Serve the food.

These aren't just ancient instructions. They are a way of life. They are, in fact, pointing to *the* way of life.

So wherever you go from here — whether you crack open Exodus next week or jump into the New Testament — I hope you carry one thing with you from our time in Genesis. Not a theology or a framework or a set of principles. Just this:

The God who spoke light into darkness in Genesis 1:3 is still speaking. The Spirit that hovered over the void is still hovering over yours. And one day — maybe in this life, maybe in the next — the hovering will end, love will strike the emptiness, and everything sad is going to come untrue.

That's not the end of the story. That's the beginning.

Thanks for walking through Genesis with me. God bless you and yours — abundantly, deeply, and amidst whatever chaos you find yourself in.

"In the beginning, God..." (Genesis 1:1)

"I am making everything new." (Revelation 21:5, NIV)

About the author

Josh Wood is a native of Amarillo, Texas. He and his wife, Careese, are graduates of Texas A&M University (Gig 'em). Josh went on to obtain his MBA from Baylor University (Sic 'em).

Newly wedded Josh and Careese made a number of definitive statements regarding their future, including the following classics: "We'll never move back to Amarillo." "We'll have three or four kids. Those kids will never throw fits in Walmart." "We'll never home school our children." "Home churches are weird."

They live in Amarillo. They have ten kids. They home school. They started a home church. They've wiped numerous tears off the Walmart floor. Their hobbies include raising children and trying to avoid definitive statements about their future.

Keep up with Josh on social media. He's @joshwoodtx on Instagram, Facebook, X, Substack, YouTube, and Threads. This book is available via podcast wherever you get your podcasts. Just search "Josh Wood's Genesis Podcast."

www.ingramcontent.com/pod-product-compliance
Lightning Source LLC
Chambersburg PA
CBHW032012050726
47590CB00006B/2137